PUBLICATIONS

PAQUETTE

1st Edition
Abridged Version

Complex Limited Power of Attorney

Power of Attorney (POA only) for
Your Estate Planning Needs

Paul M. Paquette

FIRST EDITION (Abridged Version)

Ⓒ

2018, 2019

Book Design:	Paul M. Paquette	**Proofread:**	Paul M. Paquette	**CD/USB:**	Paul M. Paquette
Front Cover:	Paul M. Paquette	**Editor:**	Paul M. Paquette	**Printing:**	N/A
Back Cover:	Paul M. Paquette	**Glossary:**	Paul M. Paquette	**Company:**	Paquette Publications
Cover Photo:	Marcela	**Index:**	N/A	**Location:**	Auburn, KY - USA

Author: Paquette, Paul M.

Title: Complex Limited Power of Attorney

Subtitle: Power of Attorney (POA Only) For Your Estate Planning Needs

Identifiers: 978-1-948389-74-7 PB | 978-1-948389-96-9 HC | 978-1-948389-85-3 EBK: PDF |

Classification: Unabridged LCCN: 2018900393 | DDC: 346.7302/9—dc23 |

Subject: 1. Law | 2. Power of Attorney | 3. Practical Guides | 4. Estate Planning

PCIP:
Paquette, Paul., 1982 –
Complex Limited Power of Attorney:
Power of Attorney (POA Only) For Your Estate Planning Needs (Estate Planning Series)
by Paul Paquette --1st ed.--Auburn, KY.: Paquette Publications. c2018, c2019
ISBN - 13: 978-1-948389-74-7 (PB).   -- ISBN - 13: 978-1-948389-96-9 (HC).
ISBN - 13: 978-1-948389-85-3 (EBK: PDF).
1. Power of attorney--United States--Popular works. 2. Power of attorney--United States--Forms.
3. Estate Planning--United States--Popular works.   4. Estate planning--United States--Forms. I. Title II. Series

Special Note: Previously Titled as "**Complex Power of Attorney.**"

Summary: The book consists of (**01**) one Complex Power of Attorney (**Limited**). This Power of Attorney has an estate planning focus that provides options, depth, and flexibility while maintaining uniformity with built-in and optional safety features.

Publication Media: Paquette Publications publishes in various formats (print, electronic, and print-on-demand). Some independent purchases or material included with the standard print versions may not be available in e-books or print-on-demand. If physical media (CD, DVD, or USB Drive) is not available within the book, then said files are downloadable online in digital format.

Digital Formats: Power of Attorney, Supporting Documents, Forms (Miscellaneous / Recommended), Worksheets, and Appendices are available in the following digital formats (PDF, DOCX, DOC, and ODT).

Bulk Purchases: Purchases of titles by Paquette Publications may occur in bulk for educational, business, fund-raising, or sale promotional use. For information, please email the following: **paquettepublications@gmail.com**.

Questions: Please send all questions, suggestions, comments, and permission requests to the following email: **paquettepublications@gmail.com**.

Please Note: The purpose of this Publication(s) and its design is to provide accurate and authoritative information concerning the subject matter covered. The author has striven to use simple/plain English to clarify complex issues and make understanding/comprehension usable and intuitive. Due to the changing nature of law in the United States of America, the author makes the following **Legal Disclaimers & Waivers** on page iv.

Legal Disclaimers & Waivers

Definitions of Terms: The term "Publication(s)" shall refer, but are not limited, to the following: Power of Attorney, Supporting Documents, Worksheets, Miscellaneous Forms, Recommended Forms, and Appendices.

Waiver of Damages: The Purchaser or User of this Publication(s) agrees by default and understands the following: (**01**) The Organization, Distributor, Sales Representative, Publisher, or Author makes no guarantees of any kind or nature. (**02**) The Organization, Distributor, Sales Representative, Publisher, or Author assumes no liability for any or all damages resulting from utilizing this Publication(s) or reliance thereof. (**03**) Modification of this Publication(s) is permissible to suit a particular Purchaser or User need; however, the Purchaser or User assumes all risk.

No Representation of Services: The Purchaser or User of this Publication(s) agrees by default and understands the following: (**01**) The Organization, Distributor, Sales Representative, Publisher, or Author is not engaged in rendering professional services regarding medical, financial, legal, et cetera. (**02**) This Publication(s) is not a substitute for advice from a competent licensed professional.

Forum – Selection / Jurisdiction / Governing Law: The Purchaser or User of this Publication(s) agrees by default and understands the following: (**01**) The selection for governing law, venue, forum, and jurisdiction for all litigation shall exclusively be at the locality of the Organization (State of Incorporation) or the Author (State of Residence). (**02**) The Purchaser or User waives their right to choose, object, or make claims (economic hardship, unreasonable constraints, or inconvenience) concerning the governing law, venue, forum, and jurisdiction for all litigation against the Organization, Distributor, Sales Representative, Publisher, or Author. (**03**) Furthermore, the governing law, venue, forum, and jurisdiction may be further restricted based on City and County; please refer to "Additional Terms & Conditions" for more information.

Force / Mandatory Arbitration: The Purchaser or User of this Publication(s) agrees by default and understands the following: (**01**) All litigation, claims, disputes, settlements, judgments, lawsuits, or proceedings (governmental, administrative, governmental investigation, inquiries, hearing, request, or any appeal thereof) against the Organization, Distributor, Sales Representative, Publisher, or Author shall only go through force and binding arbitration with no other alternative legal recourse. (**02**) The arbitration shall be confidential in adherence to the Commercial Arbitration Rules of the American Arbitration Association. (**03**) Any judgment on the award rendered by the Arbitrator may be entered in any court having jurisdiction thereof or having jurisdiction over the relevant party or its assets. (**04**) The arbitration shall be performed by one (**01**) mutually agreed upon Arbitrator with experience in contract law. The arbitration shall be in English. (**05**) The Purchaser or User shall bear their costs in the arbitration with no right or award for reimbursement.

Injunctive Relief: The Purchaser or User agrees by default and understands that unauthorized access to or use of this Publication(s) that violates the limited or commercial license shall result in injunctive remedies (or an equivalent type of urgent legal relief) in any jurisdiction without providing notice or opportunity to cure.

Aggregate Liability: The Purchaser or User of this Publication(s) agrees by default and understands that the total aggregate liability arising out of or in connection with your use of or inability to use the Paquette Publications websites or Content contained thereon (whether in contract, tort, or otherwise) shall not exceed the monetary amount received by the Organization, Distributor, Sales Representative, Publisher, or Author from the Purchaser or User.

Class Action Waiver: The Purchaser or User of this Publication(s) agrees by default and understands the following: (**01**) To bring only claims in an individual capacity, not as a Class Member/Plaintiff/Petitioner in any class, consolidation, or proceeding (mass or representative). (**02**) The Arbitrator shall not consolidate more than one person's claim nor preside over any form of class, consolidation, or proceeding (mass or representative) unless the Defendant/Respondent agrees in writing to such actions in advance.

Additional Terms & Conditions: The Purchaser or User of this Publication(s) agrees by default and understands that their legal and consumer rights are restricted and legally bound to any/all updated Additional Terms & Conditions set forth on **www.paquettepublications.com** without prior or future notice. The Additional Terms & Conditions URL links are at the bottom of the home page: Legal Disclaimers & Waivers, License & Trademark, and All Rights Reserved.

Note of Caution: When filling out this Publication(s), please consider the following. The Purchaser or User should seek a legal professional's advice if the Purchaser or User is less than eighteen (18) years of age and currently deemed mentally incompetent or incapacitated. Feel free to utilize this Publication(s) as a template. However, without legal representation in the situation above, this Publication(s) would suffer litigation by Interested Third Parties and more than likely receive judgment as invalid. Remember, an active lawful court order covering the subject matter within this Publication(s) will always take precedence if a conflict occurs. **Please Note:** If the Purchaser or User does have an active court order. The Purchaser or User can design this Publication(s), so it is not in conflict; however, seek the advice of a legal professional if there are any questions.

Legal Questions: Practicing law without a license is a crime that comes with some hefty fines in the United States of America. To avoid the appearance of impropriety, the Author will not dispense any legal advice or provide any legal services. Furthermore, no Author of any self-help legal book will willfully give legal advice or services due to liability reasons. If the Purchaser or User has a legal question(s), seek out the advice of a competent licensed Attorney.

PUBLICATIONS

A
Q
U
E
T
T
E

"Nothing is impossible to him who will try." ~ Alexander the Great

Paul M. Paquette

Is a Western Kentucky University alumnus with a Financial Planning and Management degree.

He is a military veteran in the United States Army with eight years of experience as a Financial Management Technician.

Insurance & Securities License.

Free Thinker & Entrepreneur.

Favorite hobbies include coin collecting, watching movies, genealogy, camping, hiking, fishing, reading, and cooking.

"Life is really simple, but we insist on making it complicated." ~ Confucius

Overview & Perspective

Importance of Agent(s) Selection: In the Author's opinion, a Power of Attorney (POA) is the most powerful legal document a person can execute for estate planning purposes. Thus, the Principal should think long and hard when choosing an Agent. The Principal should seek a **Reliable, Trustworthy,** and **Competent** Agent(s). Do not shirk in doing one's due diligence regarding Agent selections; if doubts or concerns exist, suggest utilizing the various optional safety features available within the POA.

Categories of POA: The Author breaks down a POA into the following four categories: (**01**) Simple, (**02**) Complex, (**03**) Durable, and (**04**) Special. A **Simple POA** is for short-term (less than five years) use with an Agent whose honor is beyond reproach and doubt. A **Complex POA** is for long-term (greater than five years) use, preferably with multiple Agents to reflect the changing realities of life with optional safety features that create additional administrative burdens but with checks and balances on the Agent's power. A **Durable POA** is, in essence, a Complex POA; however, the durability provisions are already active. A **Special POA** is, in essence, a Simple POA best used spartanly with a limited scope and purpose.

Various Type of POA: Within the various categories of POA are the following types that the Author has written or plans to write so far:
- **Simple POA:** (**01**) Limited, (**02**) Banking, (**03**) Financial, (**04**) General, (**05**) Real Estate, and (**06**) Minor.
- **Complex POA:** (**01**) Limited, (**02**) Banking, (**03**) Financial, (**04**) General, (**05**) Real Estate, and (**06**) Minor.
- **Durable POA:** (**01**) Protecting, (**02**) Final Disposition, (**03**) Health Care, and (**04**) Health Care of Minor.
- **Special POA:** (**01**) Taxes, (**02**) Vehicles, and (**03**) Pets.

Principal: A Principal is a person who establishes a POA. The Principal names an Agent and bestows that person the ability to perform actions on the Principal's behalf.

Agent: An Agent serves in a fiduciary capacity on behalf of the Principal. This fiduciary position is usually voluntary. Monetary compensation and reimbursement usually occur if the Principal has the financial means. The POA outlines the Agent's powers along with any goals and objectives.

Delegate: A Delegate (non-acting Agent) serves on behalf of the acting Agent currently in power. This discretionary power is useful when the acting Agent suffers inconveniences due to a lack of knowledge, logistics issues, or time constraints. This optional safety feature is only available for Complex and Durable POAs.

Protector: A Protector safeguards the best interest/wishes of the Principal (primarily in a passive capacity) and provides basic administrative support (ensuring transparency) to the Agent. However, if the Agent violates their role as a Fiduciary, it is the role of the Protector to step in, relieve the Agent, and protect the Principal's rights and interests. To utilize a Protector, a Durable Protecting POA must proactively occur first to bestow such power to the Agent who shall serve as a Protector. This optional safety feature is only available for Complex and Durable POAs.

Supporting Documents: These supporting documents accompany the POA for administrative purposes; these documents are optional (may be required). The Agent's forms are as follows: (**01**) **Acknowledgment of Appoint by Agent,** (**02**) **Acknowledgment of Resignation by Agent,** (**03**) **Affidavit of Full Force and Effect,** (**04**) **Delegation of Agent's Power,** (**05**) **Revocation of Delegate by Agent,** and (**06**) **Co-Agent Agreement.** The Principal's forms are as follows: (**01**) **Revocation in Whole,** (**02**) **Revocation in Part(s),** (**03**) **Revocation of Agent,** and (**04**) **Revocation of Delegate by Principal.** The Protector's forms are as follows: (**01**) **Acknowledgment of Appoint by Protector,** (**02**) **Acknowledgment of Resignation by Protector,** (**03**) **Revocation of Agent by Protector,** and (**04**) **Revocation of Delegate by Protector.** The Delegate's forms are as follows: (**01**) **Acknowledgment of Appoint by Delegate** and (**02**) **Acknowledgment of Resignation by Delegate.**

Forms Miscellaneous: These forms are available for the Principal; however, they are optional. Each document can stand alone and be extremely useful; think of it as an administrative support document that will make the Agent's life easier. These forms are as follows: (**01**) **Statement of Wishes,** (**02**) **Personal Information Worksheet,** (**03**) **Notification / Contact List,** (**04**) **Personal Documents Locator,** and (**05**) **Legal Document Locator.**

Forms Recommended: These forms are available for the Principal; however, they are optional. Each document can stand alone and be extremely useful; think of it as an administrative support document that will make the Agent's life easier. These forms are (**01**) **Affidavit of Principal's Health State** and (**02**) **Assets & Liabilities Worksheet.**

Appendices: These appendices are available for the Principal; however, these documents are optional (may be required). Each appendix can stand alone and be extremely useful; think of it as an administrative support document that will make the Agent's life easier. These appendices are as follows: (**01**) **Appendix A: Insurance Suggestions & Resource Guide,** (**02**) **Appendix B: Directions for Prudent & Safe Investing,** (**03**) **Appendix C: Attorney Suggestions & Resource Guide,** and (**04**) **Appendix D: Steps for Credit Repair & Statute of Limitations.**

PUBLICATIONS

AQUETTE

"Whoever is trying to bring you down is already below you." ~ Ziad K. Abdelnou

Be Pragmatic - Not Idealistic

The Principal should take great stride in being practical, especially regarding the nature of Power, Money, Time Management, and Motivation. Just because the Principal writes down what they want an Agent to do and bestows power to an Agent does not mean that the Principal's objectives will occur. For the Principal's objective to become a reality, there must be proper incentives or a great underlying sense of duty and honor. The Principal should read the topics below and evaluate their estate-planning situation realistically. Failure to do so otherwise will result in disaster.

Communication: Before drafting a Power of Attorney (**POA**), the Principal should take the time and make a phone call to the potential Agent(s) to verify if the Agent(s) are willing to act on the Principal behalf in a fiduciary manner. **Rhetorical Questions:** What is the point of appointing an Agent in a POA if the Agent declines to act later?

Administrative: When implementing a POA, make sure that all Agent(s) have an Original Notarized POA for their personal use in their possession. Failure to provide each Agent(s) with an Original Notarized POA will prevent or hinder their ability to execute the Principal's goals, objectives, and wishes. If the Agent(s) is completely unaware of the Principal's POA existence, do not expect anything to occur. A POA is useless if placed in a dresser drawer; remember to give the POA to the Agent(s).

Most businesses and institutions want to see the original notarized POA before letting the Agent(s) act for the Principal. The business or institution will usually make a copy of the original notarized POA for their file.

Transparency: Transparency begins with the Principal. If the Principal only provides POA to one of the Agents but not the others, it is foolhardy to expect an Agent to make copies and inform other Agent(s) and Third Parties of the Principal's POA.

Knowledge is power; an Agent will most likely not inform other legitimate Third Parties of the limits of their power. Thus, transparency is paramount to equalize the knowledge deficit that may exist and prevent such abuse of power.

Financial Resources: Do not expect an Agent(s) to perform out of the kindness of their heart and from their pockets. Be prepared to monetary reimburse the Agent(s) for their time and effort.

If the Principal wants specific actions to occur, ensure financial resources are available to achieve those objectives. Do not expect the Agent(s) to finance and pay for the Principal's objectives and wishes.

Write Clearly: When writing provisions and directives within the POA, the Principal must accomplish the following:
(01) The Principal must write clearly, as to what the Principal wants the Agent(s) to achieve;
(02) The Principal must not be vague, inconsistent, or conflicting about their intent and desires.

Co-Agents: **Current Situation:** When deciding to use Co-Agents (only available for Complex and Durable POA) as a form of checks and balances, the Principal would be wise to consider the following:

Questions to Ask: Do the Co-Agents have issues with one another? Have the Co-Agents ever worked together; if so, were there any issues or conflicts? Are there known social issues or grievances between the Co-Agents? Are the relationship dynamics between the Co-Agents confrontational, thus hindering the Principal's POA objectives?

Rhetorical Questions: What is the point of having Co-Agents, especially if both Agents have issues working together?

Pragmatic Reality: If Co-Agents cannot work together, instead of protecting the Principal's interests, the Co-Agents are more likely to prevent actions from occurring, thus delaying the Principal's wishes. When time is of the essence - this is usually detrimental.

Delegate: **Current Situation:** When deciding to use Delegate (only available for Complex and Durable POA), the Principal would be wise to consider the following:

Questions to Ask: Does the Principal have property or assets in more than one physical location? Do certain Agents have specific skill sets that other Agents do not process?

Rhetorical Questions: If an Agent defers some of their responsibility to a Delegate, will the Principal have issues with that?

Pragmatic Reality: Consider using a Delegate if the Principal current situation is complex. The more flexibility the Agent(s) has in implementing the Principal's objectives. The more likely, those objectives will become a reality.

Protector: **Current Situation:** When deciding to use Protector (only available for Complex and Durable POA) as a form of checks and balances, the Principal would be wise to consider the following:

Questions to Ask: Does the Principal have trust issues with any of the Agent(s) selected for the POA? Does the Principal believe that a Protector has enough willpower and devotion to keep the Agent(s) in check from exceeding their power and authority? Will the Protector be a pawn or bend to an Agent's will?

Rhetorical Questions: What is the point of having a Protector if the Protector decides not to enforce the terms and conditions of the POA to the best of their ability? Will the Protector be impartial and independent when using their powers?

Pragmatic Reality: If the Principal is considering a Protector to police the Agent's actions regarding the POA, then the Agent(s) for consideration are slim pickings. It will be highly advantageous to reconsider the Agent(s) selection. Consider only having one (**01**) Protector in charge that can make unilateral decisions versus hamstringing the Agent with Co-Agency. Most importantly, ensure the Principal selects the right Agent to serve as the Protector.

PUBLICATIONS
AQUETTE

"Challenges are what make life interesting and overcoming them is what make life meaningful." ~ Joshua J. Marine

To my Dad,

Kenneth J.

Paquette

Thank you for

your love and

support.

Table of Contents

✝ Image Source – Art, Graphics, Illustrations, Photos
Types of POA – Explanation of the different kinds of POA
Power of Attorney – Current & Future Books by the Author
Declaration – Current & Future Books by the Author
Advance Directives – Current & Future Books by the Author
Relationship Agreements – Current & Future Books by the Author
Technical Support – Word Programs, PDF Editors, and Printers
Downloadable Digital Files – PDF, DOCX, DOC, ODT
CD / DVD – Page allocated for Sleeve & CD / DVD

This page is intentionally left blank

CHAPTER 01

Introductions

CHAPTER 01

Overview

Introductions

Overview

Chapter 01 provides the opportunity for the Author to communicate directly with the Reader (Purchaser or User) regarding the purpose and goals of this book. Furthermore, the Author briefly comments on the positive and negative attributes that the Reader (Purchaser or User) may encounter when using a self-help law book (Growing Trends, Cost/Value Analysis, Local Rules, Law Dynamics, and Legal Research).

- **Purpose of this Book**   **(0.4 Pages Total)**
  Self-explanatory - outlines the author's primary motivation and answers the "why" question.

- **Goal of this Book**   **(0.2 Pages Total)**
  Self-explanatory - outlines the author's goal and states what the author is trying to achieve.

- **Using Self – Help Law Books**   **(0.1 Pages Total)**
  Highlights the advantages and disadvantages of doing one's legal work and expands on the topic below to include the following: Growing Trend, Cost / Value Analysis, Local Rules, and Changes in the Law.

- **Growing Trends**   **(0.3 Pages Total)**
  The author's commentary explains why doing one's legal work has become a growing trend in today's society.

- **Cost / Value Analysis**   **(0.4 Pages Total)**
  The author's commentary explains the economic benefits and value of doing one's legal work.

- **Local Rules**   **(0.2 Pages Total)**
  The author's commentary explains how local rules can potentially affect a legal document's execution and legitimacy.

- **Law Dynamics**   **(0.2 Pages Total)**
  The author's commentary explains how laws serve society and how the evolution of laws reflects society's needs.

- **Legal Research**   **(0.2 Pages Total)**
  The author's commentary explains how to perform and research legal issues using various methodologies.

Purpose of this Book

In the Author's humble opinion and experience, most people need "living" legal documents that can adjust and "provide for breathing room" over time, with practical concepts and applications relevant to everyday life.

Through research and experience, the Author has analyzed numerous legal forms, with the majority sharing the following characteristics: (**01**) lack of detail and depth, (**02**) lack of options, and (**03**) very narrow in purpose or scope, especially when the subject matter is broad and vast. These deficiencies are primarily due to legal forms being locality or state-specific, usually deriving from the statutory form that had to meet the approval of some committee in which agendas (political, religious, and lobbyist) dictate available options. These statutory forms typically give a courteous overview of the subject matter in question without addressing the finer details and permeable conditions that one usually encounters in life. The lack of personal rights and liberties offer in statutory forms leaves little in the way of protection.

When Attorneys draft legal forms, these forms are usually premade with boilerplate language. Unless the client explicitly asks the Attorney to include specifics to address the eventualities that may occur with protective language in a disaster, said safety features are invisible. The lack of protectionism and detail is primarily due to the Attorney's inherent conflict of getting the job done in the least amount of time possible to maximize profits. Conversely, a client is usually unwilling to pay a high legal fee to compensate the Attorney for the time necessary to make said legal document "Iron Clad." A financial equilibrium develops when drafting a legal document with the unspoken agreement of "hey, this may not work in all life situations." Thus, the client may have to consult with an Attorney yet again and spend more money if an unanticipated situation occurs.

Power of Attorney is the focus of this book; within this book is (**01**) one Complex Power of Attorney (**Limited**). This Power of Attorney has an estate planning focus that provides options, depth, and flexibility while maintaining uniformity with built-in and optional safety features.

The Goal of this Book

The goal of the Author through this book is to provide legal forms with an estate planning focus that has options and depth while maintaining uniformity, thus offering clear directives that are flexible with built-in safety features that are inherently lacking in most legal forms.

The design of these legal forms within this book is for use in the United States of America. Use these legal forms as a template and adjust them appropriately with the help of a competent, licensed Attorney if the Purchaser or User lives in another country. These legal forms may be most applicable and adaptable to countries with a legal basis derived from Great Britain's common law approach; thus, any of Great Britain's current and former colonies are good candidates. Remember, laws from various countries differ; however, laws tend to converge to form some universal doctrine; this phenomenon has increased rapidly due to technological advancement, thus allowing for the greater exchange of ideas. **Please Note:** Not all countries are at the same convergence rate; countries with similar roots and thoughts will be closer to convergence. The disparity can be significant, especially regarding laws from two distinct and separate cultures.

The Author hopes that the goals stated in this book succeed or surpass the Purchaser's or User's expectations and give the Purchaser or User a sense of peace and security in their everyday life.

Using Self-Help Law Books

One should be aware of the inherent advantages and disadvantages of doing one's legal work. Thus, it behooves the Purchaser or User to understand the challenges and difficulties this may encompass. The Author will briefly discuss the following: Growing Trends, Cost/Value Analysis, Local Rules, Law Dynamics, and Legal Research when using self-help law books.

• Growing Trends

There has been a noticeable trend for Purchasers or Users to prepare their legal documents and handle their legal affairs versus hiring an Attorney. Courts across this country recognize that legal services are expensive and make every effort to make it easier for the individual(s) to represent themselves. However, on the reverse side of the coin, do not expect the courts to accommodate and provide sympathy for Purchaser or User who chooses not to utilize an Attorney. Some legal professionals and courts take the attitude, "want to save a buck, fine; however, if the Purchaser or User has any questions, go to the law library and figure it out."

The Author believes the Purchaser or User should have options, to make their lives easier and less confusing from a legal perspective. The Author tries to make these forms modular, universal, and easy to understand, with built-in directions. However, the Author cannot cover every conceivable possibility and include all the nuances due to local laws, statutes, and ruling. Thus, it is highly advantageous that the Purchaser or User seeks the advice of a competent, licensed State Attorney if clarification or additional help regarding legal issues is required.

• Cost / Value Analysis

The global marketplace offers many options when shopping for a product or service with various quality levels and price points. When deciding on purchasing a product or service, the Purchaser or User will internally make a cost/value analysis base on their willingness to pay for the desired quality.

Most legal situations are straightforward and require a simple form, no complex analysis, some intelligence, and the ability to follow instructions. In situations like these, it makes sense to do one's legal work to save money at the expense of a small amount of the Purchaser's or User's time. However, in special or unique situations that are incredibly complex, a personal approach is prudent; seek a licensed attorney who can provide such service. Do not be cheap, realize one's limitations, and admit when help is required.

Creating a self-help law book involving legal matters entails simplifying the laws and condensing several legal cases into a single sentence or paragraph. Due to such simplifications, complications may arise that only an Attorney will notice. Remember, this is not a law book; if it were, it would be about a thousand pages long and too complex for most people to understand. The simplification process does entail leaving out many details and nuances that may apply to unique or unusual situations. Depending on whose opinion and specialty, there may be several valid interpretations for a legal principle or basis; thus, the possibility exists that a Judge may disagree with the Author's analysis.

Therefore, when deciding to utilize a self-help law book and do one own legal work, a cost/value analysis occurs. The Purchaser or User has to decide to save money (money spent on an Attorney instead) by doing the legal work themself, thus calculating that their efforts will outweigh the chances of rejection for their case (legal matters). Most individuals deciding to handle their legal affairs never encounter a legal problem, but occasionally people find that it costs more to have an Attorney fix their problem than to hire an Attorney to deal with it in the beginning. The Author is not trying to dissuade the Purchaser or User from legal empowerment but only to disclose the risk when handling one's legal matters. Consult with a competent, licensed State Attorney if the Purchaser or User has any questions or needs guidance.

• Local Rules

This book is not all-inclusive; there are limitations regarding what a self-help law book can do for the Purchaser or User. One should be aware that there are bound to be procedural differences that vary from state to state, county to county, and potentially even Judge to Judge. The Purchaser or User should not expect to be able to get all the information and resources solely from within the confines of this book or any book. However, this book will serve as a guide to give the Purchaser or User-specific information whenever possible to help find out what else the Purchaser or User may need to know.

It is highly advantageous that before using any of the forms within this book, the Purchaser or User consults with their court clerk. The court clerks will inform the Purchaser or User if there are any local rules or forms that one should be aware of that are required. Usually, these forms will require the same information as the forms within this book but merely format differently, with slightly different wording, or using different color paper so that the clerk can quickly locate the document. The court clerk may ask for additional information to process the legal document.

• Law Dynamics

The law is not static and constant; it is ever-evolving and dynamic. Given enough time, social and political pressures will change the laws, thus reflecting the very fabric of our civilization, as age-old rulings are overturned and lie fallow. This book is not a reflection pool, nor is the Author a seer who can peer into the future. It behooves the Purchaser or User of this book to check for the most recent statutes, rules, and regulations to see if any changes have occurred since its publication.

In most cases, the changes in the law will be insignificant, for example, a redesigned form, extra information, or alteration to a waiting period. Thus, the Purchaser or User might need to revise a form, file another form, or wait for an additional time; these changes will not usually affect the outcome of a case / legal matter. However, significant changes occasionally happen, and the entire law in a particular area requires a new interpretation. A legal case that serves as the basis for a central legal point becomes invalid, null, or void, thus impairing the Purchaser's or User's legal goal. If there are unique local requirements or recent changes in the law, seek the advice of a competent, licensed Attorney.

• Legal Research

If the Purchaser or User needs additional information, consult the local law library, usually found at the county courthouse or a law school. Ask the librarian for assistance concerning the subject matter of interest. The primary source of information will be in the State's Statutes or Codes, with titles such as "Revised" or "Annotated" the title may include the publisher's name, and there could be more than one publisher. Ensure the Purchaser or User has the current version of their State laws. The most common way to update law books is a soft-cover supplement found on the back of each volume; other methods include supplement volume, loose-leaf bindings, and supplement sections. An additional source of legal information is as follows: Internet Research (suggests visiting **www.findlaw.com**); Practice manuals; Digest (gives summaries of appeals court cases); Case Reporter (contains full written opinions of appeals court cases); and Legal Encyclopedia (Major sets include *American Jurisprudence* and *Corpus Juris Secundum*).

CHAPTER 02

Instructions

CHAPTER 02

Overview

Instructions

Overview

The following are stand-alone instructional pages for convenience purposes only; each document within this chapter comes with built-in instructions for easy completion. These stand-alone instructional pages may help clarify questions or provide additional insights that the Reader (Purchaser or User) may have.

- ### POA's Legal Requirement   (01 Pages Total)
  The author explains the legal requirements, justifications, and prudent measures for the Principal, Witnesses, and Notary within the United States of America.

- ### Instructions for Principal   (01 Pages Total)
  This (stand-alone) instructional page guides the Principal as to what their requirements are when it comes to filling out a Power of Attorney (Simple, Complex, Durable, and Special) within this book.

- ### Instructions for Witnesses   (01 Pages Total)
  This (stand-alone) instructional page guides the Witnesses as to what their requirements are when it comes to filling out a Power of Attorney (Simple, Complex, Durable, and Special) within this book.

- ### Instructions for Notary Public   (01 Pages Total)
  This (stand-alone) instructional page guides the Notary Public as to what their requirements are when it comes to filling out a Power of Attorney (Simple, Complex, Durable, and Special) and Supporting Documents within this book.

- ### Built-In Safety Features   (06 Pages Total)
  These (stand-alone) instructional pages highlight the Built-in Safety Feature found in the Power of Attorney (Simple, Complex, Durable, and Special) within this book.

- ### Optional Safety Features   (06 Pages Total)
  These (stand-alone) instructional pages highlight the Optional Safety Feature found predominately in this book's Power of Attorney (Complex and Durable).

POA's Legal Requirements

Not A Court Order:

A Power of Attorney (**POA**) is not a court order; the execution of this POA is strictly voluntary; implementation of the POA **must be proactive to be effective and valid**. Falsification of this POA may constitute a criminal offense.

Recordation:

It is highly advantageous (more acceptable to bank officials or other financial institutions) that the Principal record/file (usually optional) the POA with the courts/official state record keeper, usually at the county level known as "county recorder of deeds." Utilizing a POA for Real Estate Transactions will require recordation and a Thumb/Finger Print in the Execution and Signature Page. It is advisable to consult with a licensed Attorney or the County Recorder of Deeds if there are any special filing/recording requirements.

Various State Laws:

As of 2011, every State within the U.S.A. has enacted the Uniform Power of Attorney Act (UPOAA) except for Louisiana; however, each State may have differences concerning the legal requirements relating to the execution of a POA. All States require that the Principal (the person enacting the POA) sign and date the POA. Depending upon the State, the requirements for Witnesses are the following: (**01**) one or more Witnesses, (**02**) two Witnesses and a Notary Public, or (**03**) either two Witnesses or a Notary Public. In States where both a Witnesses and a Notary Public are requirements, some States require notarization of only the Principal's signature. In contrast, other states require notarization of the Principal and both Witnesses. Free notary services are usually within a Government Facility, Post Office, or Public Libraries.

Legal Prudence:

Due to the various legal requirements of each State, the POA within this book conforms to the most prudent of measures concerning Principal, Witnesses, and Notary Public requirements. Thus, every POA within this book requires the Principal Signature and Date, (**02**) two Witnesses Signature and Date, and a Notary Public attestation to the Principal and Witnesses Signature and Date, along with the Notary Public's Seal, Signature, and Date. By notarizing the POA, the Principal has made it extremely difficult for a Third Party to challenge the validity of the Principal's signature and intentions.

Principal Requirements:

Although not all states require the following concerning the Principal, it is a prudent practice that the Principal meets the following criteria to execute a POA (to prevent future legal challenges). (**01**) The Principal is at least eighteen (**18**) years or older. (**02**) The Principal is of sound and disposing mind (emotionally and mentally competent). (**03**) The Principal has the capacity with full memory or necessary mental faculties. (**04**) The Principal willfully and voluntarily executes this POA. **Please Note:** If the Principal is old and may exhibit signs of functioning non-socially, incapacitated, or incompetent in the future, it is highly advantageous that the Principal proactively implements an **Affidavit of Principal's Health State** before implementing a POA.

Witnesses and Notary Public Requirements:

Although not all states require the following concerning the Witnesses and Notary Public, it is a prudent practice that the Witnesses and Notary Public do not have a conflict of interest and thus be impartial during the execution process of the POA (this is to prevent future legal challenges). These criteria will be grounds for a conflict of interest if the Witnesses or Notary Public is one or more: (**01**) Any individual related to the Principal by blood, marriage, or adoption. (**02**) Any individual who is currently a Beneficiary of the Principal's estate (laws of intestate succession or any existing will/codicil). (**03**) Any individual who benefits from a financial policy (insurance or annuity), in which the Principal's life is the insured. (**04**) Any individual claiming (present/inchoate) any portion of the Principal's estate. (**05**) Any individual who serves as an Owner, Operator, or employee of a Health Care Facility (Medical, Mental, Assisted Living), in which the Principal is currently a Patient / Client unless the employee serves solely as a Notary Public. (**06**) Any Doctor, Physician, Psychologist, Psychiatrist, Social Worker, Financial Advisor, and Financial Manager in which the Principal is currently a Patient / Client. (**07**) Any individual who serves as an Owner, Operator, or employee of a Final Dispositional Facility (Funerary Home, Crematory Authority, and Cemetery Authority) unless the employee serves solely as a Notary Public. (**08**) Any individual who is an Agent (active/inactive) serving in a fiduciary capacity under this POA. (**09**) Upon the Principal death, any individuals or entities may have a claim (the creditor) against the Principal's estate. (**10**) Any individual under the age of eighteen (**18**) years or is currently incapacitated or incompetent. The Witnesses should be twenty-one (**21**) years of age or older.

Benefits:

The above requirements may seem burdensome and overzealous on the Author's part to impose upon the Principal, especially if the State of residency does not require all of these extra precautions; however, the end benefits are well worth it. By enacting these prudent measures concerning the Principal, Witnesses, and Notary --- companies, third-party service providers, and professionals (Doctors, Attorneys, Financial Advisers, et cetera) are more likely to honor the POA without questions. If the invocation of the POA was to occur in another State, the Principal could rest peacefully knowing that their POA would be just as effective and legitimate in that State.

Revocation:

When revoking a POA, two (**02**) Witnesses and a Notary Public are preferred; however, a Notary Public is a bare minimum requirement. Furthermore, a current **Affidavit of Principal's Health State** accompanying the Revocation is highly advantageous, especially if legally challenged in the future. All Revocation documents within this book require notarization.

Instructions

© 2018 by Paul M. Paquette; Form v3.00
All Rights Reserved; Paquette Publications

Power of
Attorney

Must verify Agent Identity with
a Government Issue Picture I.D.

Page 01 of 01

Instructions for Principal

A Principal is a person who implements (fills out and executes) a legal document (Power of Attorney) that gives power to another person named the Agent to interact with and create a legal arrangement with a Third Party.

Fill out the Identifying Information of the Key Individual (Principal, Agent, Protector):

Key Individual →

Full Name:
Address:
Phone #: Email:
Residence: County: State:

The following are selection choices in various formats that the Principal will encounter throughout the Power of Attorney.

"Y" or "N" Here ↑ Initial Here ↑

Place "Y" for Yes or "N" for No in the box and initial "✒" the line if the Principal desires the following:

(A) Effective Immediately

Place a "✓" in the box if the Principal desires the following:

Report Period: ☐ None ☐ Monthly ☐ Quarterly ☐ Annually

The Principal wants to establish an expiration date for this POA as stated below:

The date that POA Expires: Month of: _____ Day of: _____ Year of: _____

Fill out the Identifying Information of the Principal as shown in Signature and Execution:

Principal →

Full Legal Name:

Today's Date:

Signature: ✒

Thumb/Finger Print:

Real Estate Transaction

Optional Safety Feature: At the bottom of **each** page of the Legal document is a security device reference as the Security Footer; if the **Security Footer** setting is to **"Low," "Moderate,"** or **"High,"** then the **Principal** needs to initial the bottom of each page as designated below for that page to be valid and enforceable.

1ˢᵗ **Witness:** _____ 2ⁿᵈ **Witness:** _____ **Notary Public:** _____ **Principal:** ↙ _____

Instructions for Witnesses

A Witness(es) is a person(s) who signs their name to the legal documents for attestation purposes concerning the authenticity that the Principal has authorized a course of action.

The role of the Witness is to verify that the Principle is 18 years of age or older, has created said legal document, and did so of their free choice while in a state of mental and emotional competency. When selecting a witness, the criteria are as follows: 18 years or older (prefer 21 years), cannot benefit directly or indirectly from the Principal, unbiased party, and no immediate relation to the Principal. On the **Signature and Execution Page** is the following regarding the (02) two Qualified Adult Witnesses.

Have (02) two Adult Witness* the Principal's signature in addition to having their signature notarized*

In the joint presence of each other, the Witnesses State that the Principal is the following: **(01)** The Principal is at least eighteen **(18)** years or older. **(02)** The Principal is of sound and disposing mind (emotionally and mentally competent). **(03)** The Principal is not suffering from constraint, duress, fraud, or undue influence. **(04)** The Principal acknowledges having willfully and voluntarily dated and signed this POA (or asked/directed for such actions to occur). **(05)** The Witnesses affirm that they have no direct biological or marital relationship with the Principal and are not a Beneficiary of the Principal's estate. **(06)** The Witnesses affirm their impartiality and confirm that the criterion stated in the box at the bottom of the last page does not apply. **(07)** The Witnesses declare this paragraph true and correct under the Penalty of Perjury.

If the Witness is uncomfortable giving out personal contact information, current employment information and occupation will suffice.

1st Witness →

Name:		Signature:
Address:		
Phone #:		
Occupation:		Date:

2nd Witness Or Special Witness ** →

Name:		Signature:
Address:		
Phone #:		
Occupation:		Date:

Optional Safety Feature: At the bottom of **each** page of the Legal document is a security device reference as the Security Footer; if the **Security Footer** setting is "**High**," then the two **(02) Witness** need to initial the bottom of each page as designated below for that page to be valid and enforceable.

1st Witness: _____   **2nd Witness:** _____   **Notary Public:** _____   **Principal:** _____

© 2018 by Paul M. Paquette; Form v3.00
All Rights Reserved; Paquette Publications

Power of
Attorney

Must verify Agent Identity with
a Government Issue Picture I.D.

Page 01 of 01

Instructions for Notary Public

A Notary Public is a public officer constituted by law to serve the public in non-contentious matters. Whose primary functions are to (01) administer oaths/affirmations and (02) witness and authenticate the executions of the legal documents.

The Notary Public's role is to verify that the Principle is 18 years of age or older, has created said legal document, and did so of their free choice while in a state of mental and emotional competency. Furthermore, the Notary Public shall attest that witnesses have signed this document in their presence. When selecting a Notary Public, the criteria are as follows: 18 years or older (prefer 21 years), cannot benefit directly or indirectly from the Principal, unbiased party, and no immediate relation to the Principal. On the **Signature and Execution Page** is the following that relates to the Notary Public.

UNDER THE LAWS OF →

COUNTY: _____

STATE: _____

Before the Notary Public (the undersigned authority) comes forth, the Principal, with a sound/disposed mind, is eighteen (18) years or older. The Principal acknowledges having willfully and voluntarily dated and signed this POA (or asked/directed for such actions to occur) stated above in the Notary Public presence. If Witnesses sign and attest that the Principal has signed this POA, the Notary Public shall attest that the Witnesses have signed this POA in the Notary Public's presence. Furthermore, the Notary Public states that the Principal has provided a Government Issue identification card with a facial picture to prove identity. The Notary Public declares under the Penalty of Perjury that this paragraph is true and correct.

If the Principal or Witnesses sign this POA but not in the presence of the Notary Public, then the Notary Public will not notarize or sign this POA.

* Notary Public →

Full Name:		Signature & Seal:	
Location:			
Address:			
Phone #:		I.D. Number:	
Date:		Commission Expires:	

Optional Safety Feature: At the bottom of **each** page of the Legal document is a security device reference as the Security Footer; if the **Security Footer** setting is **Moderate**" or "**High**," then the **Notary Public** needs to initial the bottom of each page as designated below for that page to be valid and enforceable.

1ˢᵗ Witness: _____   2ⁿᵈ Witness: _____   Notary Public: _____   Principal: _____

Built-In Safety Features

Built-in Safety Features

These documents come with **Built-in Safety Features** to protect the Principal; the following examples illustrate these safety features and explain why they exist.

Choice Selection: It allows the Principal to select "**Yes**" or "**No**" with either a **Y** or **N**; along with initialization, this allows for modulation and verification for choice selection.

Article III: Effective Date of POA

The Principal wants the following regarding the effective date for the legal enforcement of this POA: The Principal can choose from (**02**) two options; however, **options A** and **B** are mutually exclusive. **Option A** shall be the default option in the event of ambiguities.

Place "**Y**" for Yes or "**N**" for No in the box and initial "✐" the line if the Principal desires the following:

(A) **Effective Immediately**

"Y" or "N" Here ↑   Initial Here ↑

By designating "**Y**" for Yes, the effective date of this POA shall begin from the day of execution, as stated in **Article XXI**. If durability provision(s) are active in **Article XIV**, those provision(s) shall immediately take effect.

Place "**Y**" for Yes or "**N**" for No in the box and initial "✐" the line if the Principal desires the following:

(B) **Effective if Events are Trigger**

"Y" or "N" Here ↑   Initial Here ↑

By designating "**Y**" for Yes, the effective date of this POA shall begin when such events transpire or occur, as outlined in **Article V**: "**Springing Powers**." If durability provision(s) are active in **Article XIV**, the durability provision(s) shall be active when such events transpire, as outlined in **Article V**: "**Springing Powers**."

Agent Conflict of Interest: This Safety feature protects the Principal from conflict of interest and situations where the Principal's financial interest may be at stake.

Article VII: Designation of Agent

The Principal should only designate an Agent if that individual is **Reliable**, **Trustworthy**, and **Competent** to manage the Principal's affairs. For legal reasons, all Agents must be competent and at least eighteen (**18**) years or older. None of the following individuals (non-relative) may serve as the Principal's Agent. (**A**) Any individual who serves as an Owner, Operator, or employee of a Health Care Facility (Medical, Mental, or Assisted Living) in which the Principal is currently a Patient / Client unless the employee serves solely as a Notary Public. (**B**) Any individual who serves as an Owner, Operator, or employee of a Final Dispositional Facility (Funerary Home, Crematory Authority, and Cemetery Authority) unless the employee serves solely as a Notary Public. (**C**) Any Doctor, Physician, Psychologist, Psychiatrist, Social Worker, Financial Advisor, or Financial Manager in which the Principal is currently a Patient / Client. Automatic Revocation of the Spouse designation as Agent shall occur if the following happens: (**01**) Dissolution or annulment of the marriage. (**02**) Proceedings are currently active for Dissolution of Marriage. (**03**) The Principal currently lives in a separate physical location from their Spouse for more than (**02**) two months with the intention of a divorce. The Principal designates the following individual as the Agent, the first choice, with decision-making powers in adherence to the terms and conditions specified in this POA.

Built-in Safety Features

These documents come with **Built-in Safety Features** to protect the Principal; the following examples illustrate these safety features and explain why they exist.

Yellow Space: This Safety feature ensures that the Principal can write in additional directions or terms (conditions, prohibitions, restrictions, exceptions, additions, limitations, extensions, and special rules). Option One (**01**) requires the writing to be "**Type.**" Option Two (**02**) requires the writing to be "**Type**" or "**Legible writing in Ink**" but not both.

Option One (01):

Specify in Detail | Must be Type

Option Two (02):

Specify in Detail | Preferably Type or Legible writing in Ink

Restrictions on Agent's Power: This Safety feature protects the Principal from actions that the Agent may do that are harmful to the Principal.

Article X: Restrictions on Agent's Powers

A: Regardless of what authorization or powers bestow in **Article VII Subsection A through X,** the Agent shall not do or perform the following: **(01)** The Agent shall not make a loan to oneself, another name Agent, or a beneficiary of the Agent. **(02)** The Agent shall not take a service fee as an Agent. **(03)** The Agent shall not create, modify, or revoke a trust. **(04)** The Agent shall not use the Principal's property to fund a trust for someone other than the Principal or a trust that does not benefit the Principal greater than seventy (70%) percent. **(05)** The Agent shall not create or change a Beneficiary's interest in the Principal's property. **(06)** The Agent shall not create or change the Principal's interest in the Principal's property solely for the benefit of another. **(07)** The Agent shall not designate or change the designation of beneficiaries to receive any property, benefit, or contract right on the Principal's death. **(08)** The Agent shall not make or revoke a gift of the Principal property in trust or another arrangement. **(09)** The Agent shall not make or revoke a gift on the Principal behalf. **(10)** The Agent shall not exercise any powers that would cause the Principal's assets to become taxable to the Agent or the Agent's estate for any income, estate, or inheritance tax. **(11)** The Agent shall not forgive debts owed to the Principal, disclaim, or waive benefits payable to the Principal. **(12)** The Agent shall not execute, publish, declare, amend, or revoke the following: last will, codicil, or any will substitute on the Principal's behalf. **(13)** The Agent shall not perform duties under a contract that requires the Principal's services. **(14)** The Agent shall not make an affidavit about the Principal's knowledge that is unknown to the Agent personally. **(15)** The Agent shall not vote in any governmental public election on behalf of the Principal unless the Agent has a notarized letter stating who the Principal's candidates and voting preferences are regarding that public election. **(16)** The Agent shall not exercise powers and authority granted to the Principal as Trustee or a court-appointed Fiduciary. **(17)** The Agent shall not exercise the right to make a disclaimer on behalf of the Principal, except for a disclaimer of a detrimental transfer or acceptance made with the court's approval. **(18)** The Agent shall not enjoin (add or transfer) ownership or title to the Principal's funds or assets in the Agent's name alone. **Please Note:** Waiver of these restrictions shall only occur if the Principal grants written permission in **Article IX Subsection Y**.

Built-in Safety Features

These documents come with **Built-in Safety Features** to protect the Principal; the following examples illustrate these safety features and explain why they exist.

Additional Legal Provisions: These safety features protect the Principal.

Modifications: Ensure the document's legitimacy and integrity.

N: Modification: Changes or modifications to this POA shall not occur upon execution. If the Principal wants to change this POA, the Principal must make an entirely new one. However, revocation of any part(s) of this POA may occur if it is in writing; once a part(s) receives revocation, it shall be permanent. Alterations (strikes out, cross out, and blackouts) of any provisions or writing within this POA shall have no bearing in a court of law and shall remain active and valid as to their original intent.

Picture I.D.: Ensure the legitimacy of the Agent.

O: Picture I.D.: The Principal requires verifying the Agent's identity with a government-issued picture ID. The Principal does not require it to be current and up to date; all that the Principal requires is the ability to confirm their facial features in a picture from an official governmental source.

Governing Law: Determines which laws and jurisdiction shall take priority if a legal issue arises.

T: Governing Law: This POA shall take effect immediately as a sealed instrument and shall receive interpretation, enforcement, and governance under the State's laws where the Principal has established physical residency at the time of enforcement. The Principal requests for the honoring of this POA in any State, County, or Location in which the Principal's body or property may be, with the intention that it be valid in all jurisdictions/territories of the United States and all Foreign Nations. This POA is to receive the most liberal interpretation available to grant the appointed Fiduciary the greatest amount of decision-making discretion.

Severability / Saving Clause: This clause ensures the survival and permanency of the legal document if certain sections or provisions are illegal or invalid.

U: Severability / Saving Clause: An invalid or unenforceable provision within this POA might exist. If that occurs, the remaining provisions of this POA shall continue and be active as if said invalid or unenforceable provision did not exist. All remaining provisions shall be undisturbed to maintain their original legal meaning, force, and effect. If a court finds or deems that an invalidated or unenforceable provision will become valid if limitations exist, then such written provision shall receive a written modification by court order to limit the provision's power while maximizing the economic value and liberties granted.

Court Appointed of Guardian or Conservator: The Principal can nominate an individual in advance if the Courts decide upon a Guardian or Conservator.

X: Court Appointed Guardian or Conservator: the Principal intends by this POA to avoid a court-supervised guardianship or conservatorship. If the Principal attempts or fails to avoid a court-supervised guardianship or conservatorship. Then, the Principal requests that the Agent designated in this POA serve as Guardian or Conservator of the Principal's property and affairs. The court-appointed Guardian or Conservator shall not have the power to revoke, suspend, or terminate this POA or the Agent's powers except as specifically authorized by law. The Principal may execute the following: **"Declaration in Advance of Need for Guardianship & Conservatorship,"** if execution occurs, the Principal prefers that those individuals act in such a fiduciary capacity.

Built-in Safety Features

These documents come with **Built-in Safety Features** to protect the Principal; the following examples illustrate these safety features and explain why they exist.

Acknowledgment by the Agent: A basic overview of the Agent's Responsibility; this is to prevent the Agent from using the excuse "I did not know" and so forth. Furthermore, since this Acknowledgment is in the Power of Attorney, the Agent cannot claim ignorance regarding their fiduciary duties.

Article XV: Acknowledgment by the Agent

A: The Agent shall exercise due care and act in the Principal's best interest with the powers granted while adhering to any limitations, impositions, or specifications within this POA.

B: The Agent's foremost duty is loyalty and protection of the Principal and the Principal's interests. The Agent shall direct any benefits derived from this POA to the Principal. The Agent must avoid conflicts of interest and use ordinary skill and prudence to exercise these powers. If there is anything about this POA or the Agent's duties that the Agent does not understand, the Agent shall seek professional advice.

C: A court of competent jurisdiction has the discretion to revoke the Agent's power, especially if acting inappropriately. Thus, it behooves the Agent to exercise the bestowed powers in a fiduciary manner. The burden will be upon the Agent to prove that such acts were prudent and within a Fiduciary standard for any questionable acts. The Agent may be liable for damages and subject to criminal and civil prosecution if a court of competent jurisdiction finds that the Agent has violated their fiduciary duty.

D: The Agent has the power to abstain from using their granted powers under this POA; however, the Agent does not have the luxury of being negligent when the **Life, Safety**, and **Welfare** of the Principal are at stake. The Agent may be liable for damages, be subject to prosecution (criminal or civil), and suffer termination of powers if a court rules that the Agent has been negligent regarding their fiduciary duty under this POA to the Principal,

E: The Agent agrees to keep all monetary funds or financial assets that belong to the Principal in separate accounts from the Agent's monetary funds or financial assets. There shall be no commingling of monetary funds or financial assets to ensure simple accounting and safeguard the Principal's financial security. Furthermore, the Agent agrees to protect, conserve, and exercise prudence and caution in dealings with the Principal's monetary funds, financial assets, and all other assets of value and worth.

F: The Agent agrees to keep a complete/accurate record of all acts, disbursements, and receipts for review/inspection. The Agent agrees to provide an accounting/report to the Principal at the following time intervals (as stated below). If the Principal dies, the Executor/Administrator of the Principal's estate shall receive the accounting/report within a quarter. **Directions: Place a "✓" in the Accounting / Report Period box.**

Report Period:		None		Monthly		Quarterly		Annually

G: By default, the Agent shall not receive compensation for their authority, rights, and responsibilities; however, the Agent may receive reimbursement for reasonable and necessary expenses incurred in performing their authority, rights, and responsibilities. The Principal may compensate the Agent if the Principal desires.

H: The Agent shall disclose all actions that require written authorization by using their identity as the Agent in the following manner: (Agent's Signature) as Agent for (Principal's Name).

I: For Simple and Special POA, the Agent may resign by notifying the Principal or the Principal's Guardian or Conservator (provided a Judge appoints one). For Complex and Durable POA, the Agent may resign by notifying the Principal, Protector, Co-Agent, Successor Agent, or the Principal's Guardian or Conservator (provided a Judge appoints one). The resignation must be in writing and sent by certified mail, statutory overnight delivery (return receipt requested), or email.

J: If the Agent becomes aware of the death of the Principal who executed the POA, the Agent must notify all Third Parties as soon as practicable that the Principal has died and that this POA is no longer legitimate and effective. If Durability Provision(s) are not active or applicable, the Agent must notify all Third Parties as soon as practicable that the Principal is functioning non-socially, incapacitated, or incompetent; thus, the POA is no longer valid.

K: If the Agent resigns or ceases to represent the Principal regarding this POA, the former Agent agrees to return all property and documents to the Principal immediately.

Due to Space Limitations, Provisions L – R are not shown.

Built-in Safety Features

These documents come with **Built-in Safety Features** to protect the Principal; the following examples illustrate these safety features and explain why they exist.

Interpretation Instruction in the event of Ambiguities: It provides a set of rules to avoid litigation and determine the Principal intent if an error occurs.

Article XI: Ambiguities Interpretation Instructions

A: If a provision requires that a specific section be "Type" to be valid, failure to **"Type"** the section shall make that part invalid, null, and void.

B: If a provision requires that a specific section have the **Principal's Initial** for it to be valid, failure to initial the section shall make that part invalid, null, and void.

C: If a fillable section is **blank**, thus not typed or filled in, the legal interpretation shall be that the Principal did not intend for that section to be effective, and when it comes to interpreting that section, it shall be invalid, null, and void.

D: If a fillable section requires a **Yes "Y"** or **No "N"** and the section is blank (thus not typed or filled in), the legal interpretation shall be that the Principal did not intend for that section to be effective; therefore, it shall be **No "N."**

E: If a fillable section requires a **Yes "Y"** or **No "N;"** however, **"Yes"** or **"No"** exists instead, the legal interpretation shall be that the Principal did intend for that section to keep its legal effect and meaning.

F: If a fillable section requires a **Check "✓"** and it is blank, thus not typed or filled in, the legal interpretation shall be that the Principal did not intend for that section to be effective; therefore, not wanted.

G: If a fillable section gives multiple options that are mutually exclusive to each other in which a **Check "✓"** is required if more than one option is checked "✓" then the legal interpretation shall be that the Principal did this in error; thus when it comes to interpreting that section, the implementation shall be of the more conservative option.

H: If a fillable section requires a **Check "✓"** or "X," however a dash "—" exists instead, the legal interpretation shall be that the Principal did not intend for that section to be effective; thus, it is not wanted.

I: If a section or provision is typed with added handwritten instructions, only the "typed" section will receive consideration concerning the Principal's intentions. The rationale is simple: any person, not necessarily the Principal, can handwrite (ink in) after the fact. Due to a lack of verification, the additional handwritten instruction shall be invalid, null, and void.

J: Most state laws will void a legal document if someone writes on the surface, especially after notarization or execution. The Principal waives this right since the formalization of the POA requires it to be typed and printed; thus, any handwritten alteration concerning the altered section shall be unsubstantial and nonbearing unless an unaltered original duplicate or legitimate copy is available; only the unreadable section shall be invalid, null, and void,

K: If this POA allows handwritten statements by the Principal and there seem to be any suspicious alterations or additions (changes in handwriting style, changes in ink), such handwritten alterations or additions shall have no weight or bearing. Unless an unaltered original duplicate or legitimate copy is available, the altered section shall only be invalid, null, and void if it (the altered section) is unreadable as to its original intentions.

L: The Descriptions that follow a **Yes "Y"** or a **No "N"** Box are for clarification and informational purposes to outline the performance of duties and rights.

M: If a Third Party receives more than one active Power of Attorney regarding the Principal: **(01)** The Power of Attorney that has the most recent date shall take more precedence unless otherwise stated in **Article VII Subsection G**. **(02)** If the Principal function non-socially, incapacitated, or incompetent, then the Power of Attorney that has an active Durability Provision(s), in effect, shall take precedence. **(03)** If the Power of Attorney has the same date, then a General Power takes precedence over a Financial Power of Attorney. A Financial Power of Attorney takes precedence over a Banking Power of Attorney. A Limited Power of Attorney shall be subservient to a General, Financial, and Banking Power of Attorney if any conflicts arise. **(04)** A Protecting Power of Attorney shall stand alone and only be binding upon Complex and Durable Power of Attorney with active Protector provisions. **(05)** A Complex Power of Attorney takes precedence over a Simple Power of Attorney if any conflicts arise. **(06)** Unless otherwise specified within a Special Power of Attorney, a Special Power of Attorney shall take precedence over a Complex and Simple Power of Attorney if there are any conflicts.

Built-in Safety Features

These documents come with **Built-in Safety Features** to protect the Principal; the following examples illustrate these safety features and explain why they exist.

Witnesses and Notary Public Conflict of Interest: This Safety feature protects the Principal from conflict of interest and situations where the Principal's financial interest may be at stake.

> *** None shall serve as a Witness, Notary Public, or other qualified individual with the authority to administer oaths regarding this POA made under this section.**

(01) Any individual related to the Principal by blood, marriage, or adoption. **(02)** Any individual currently a Beneficiary of the Principal's estate (laws of intestate succession or any existing will/codicil). **(03)** Any individual who benefits from a financial policy (insurance or annuity) in which the Principal's life is insured. **(04)** Any individual claiming (present/inchoate) any part of the Principal's estate. **(05)** Any individual who serves as an Owner, Operator, or employee of a Health Care Facility (Medical, Mental, or Assisted Living) in which the Principal is currently a Patient / Client unless the employee serves solely as a Notary Public. **(06)** Any Doctor, Physician, Psychologist, Psychiatrist, Social Worker, Financial Advisor, or Financial Manager in which the Principal is currently a Patient / Client. **(07)** Any individual who serves as an Owner, Operator, or employee of a Final Dispositional Facility (Funerary Home, Crematory Authority, and Cemetery Authority) unless the employee serves solely as a Notary Public. **(08)** Any individual who is an Agent (active/inactive) serving in a fiduciary capacity under this POA. **(09)** Upon the Principal's death, any individual or entity with a claim (the creditor) against the Principal's estate. **(10)** Any individual under eighteen **(18)** years or is incapacitated or incompetent. The Witnesses should be twenty-one **(21)** years of age or older.

Special Witness** If the Principal is a resident of a sanitarium, rest home, nursing home, boarding home, et cetera, it is highly beneficial that a patient advocate or ombudsman be one of the Witnesses while executing this POA. **Legal Questions:** Consult the State laws or contact a licensed Attorney.

This page is intentionally left blank

Optional Safety Features

Optional Safety Features

These documents come with **Optional Safety Features** to protect the Principal; the following example illustrates these safety features and their purpose.

Springing Powers: It allows the Principal to have such a document be active when said action or event occurs.

Article V: Springing Powers

SAFETY FEATURE: By implementing this option, the Principal creates an administrative burden but also creates checks and balances. This option is a personal decision that the Principal must determine for their future benefit.
STATEMENT OF ACKNOWLEDGMENT: The Principal acknowledges and states that springing powers shall only occur if **Article III Option B** is active. Furthermore, the Principal dictates that one of the following scenarios below (if selected) shall transpire/occur to activate the Springing Powers of this POA.

DIRECTIONS: The Principal must **place "Y"** for **Yes** in all applicable empty box spaces below and initial "✐" on **the line** for activation of Springing Power(s). The Principal must **place "N"** for **No** to all applicable empty box spaces below **and initial "✐" the line** for no activation of Springing Power(s). Springing Power(s) will not receive activation if the empty box space or the Principal's initial is void or left blank.

"Y" or "N" Here ↑ Initial Here ↑	**Incapacitation**	The Principal health state is **Incapacitation**; read **Article VI Subsection A**.
"Y" or "N" Here ↑ Initial Here ↑	**Incompetent**	The Principal health state is **Incompetent**; read **Article VI Subsection B** for more details.
"Y" or "N" Here ↑ Initial Here ↑	**Function Non-Socially**	The Principal health state is **Function Non-Socially**; read **Article VI Subsection C** for more details.
"Y" or "N" Here ↑ Initial Here ↑	**Active Duty – Overseas or Abroad**	The Principal is on **Active Duty either overseas or abroad** for a duration that lasts longer than **(07)** seven days (proof will consist of military orders or a signed, preferably notarized, letter from the Principal).
"Y" or "N" Here ↑ Initial Here ↑	**Business Trip – Overseas or Abroad**	The Principal is on a **business trip either overseas or abroad** for a duration that lasts longer than **(07)** seven days (proof will consist of a copy of the ticket purchased or a signed, preferably notarized, letter from the Principal).
"Y" or "N" Here ↑ Initial Here ↑	**Incarcerated in Jail, Prison, Correctional Facilities**	The Principal is in **jail, prison, or any other correctional facility** where freedom of personal movement is reduced or denied (proof will consist of evidence of incarceration or a signed, preferably notarized, letter from the Principal).
"Y" or "N" Here ↑ Initial Here ↑	**Recognize as being Officially Missing**	The Principal is officially missing (proof will consist of the missing person report by the government or law enforcement authority).

Due to Space Limitations, three (03) other scenarios are not shown.

Optional Safety Features

These documents come with **Optional Safety Features** to protect the Principal; the following example illustrates these safety features and why they exist.

Co-Power Sharing for Agent: It allows the Principal to designate an Agent to check and balance another Agent's action and vice versa due to an inherent lack of complete trust in a sole Agent.

Article VIII: Agent Co-Power Sharing

SAFETY FEATURE: Implementing this option creates an administrative burden, but it also creates checks and balances. This option is a personal decision that the Principal must make for their future benefit.

	Place "Y" for Yes or "N" for No in the box and initial "✎" the line if the Principal desires the following:	**Enable Agent Co-Power Sharing**

"Y" or "N" Here ↑   Initial Here ↑

By designating "**Y**" for Yes, the Principal has enabled co-power sharing for the Agent(s), which shall initially be the first and second choice Agent. The Agent(s) shall have the authority and power to make joint decisions on the Principal behalf in a co-power-sharing arrangement. Co-power sharing involves the Agent(s) making and implementing decisions together. Every joint decision must be in writing, with both Agents approving such decisions by signature. Succession for co-power sharing shall occur when an Agent is either unable or unwilling to accept or continue the appointment as the Agent; thus, the third choice as Agent shall take the place of the departing Agent. The succession for Agent shall continue in the manner above (as illustrated when the third choice for Agent assumes powers) until every named Agent is unable or unwilling to accept or continue the appointment as Agent. Furthermore, the Agents agree to perform all their duties as follows:

A: The Agents shall collaborate and share all knowledge and activities via letter, text, phone, or email. Email is the preferred method of communication.

B: The Agents shall not change the following: Account Information, Security Questions, Log-In Screen Name or I.D., and Passwords without having both active Agents agree to such changes in advance (preferably in writing email). An Agent shall be relieved of their powers/duties if an Agent initiates such changes to prevent the other Agent from knowing what activities are occurring.

C: Transparency is paramount, thus requiring continuous active support among all Agent(s). Disclosure of account status or changes must occur to all Agents within (07) seven days before activation or deactivation. Furthermore, all account information, security settings, and password information shall be up-to-date and continuously dispersed to all Agents (active) as soon as possible via the most efficient means of communication.

D: All Agents are accountable for their actions and shall not act alone without consent or prior agreement from the other Co-Agent; failure to do so may result in criminal or civil proceedings.

Resignation:	The Agent may resign by notifying the Principal, Protector (Complex & Durable POA), Co-Agent, Successor Agent, or the Principal's Guardian. The resignation must be in writing by certified mail, statutory overnight delivery (return receipt requested), or email.

Optional Safety Features

Only Complex and Durable Power of Attorneys come with **Optional Safety Features** to protect the Principal; the following example illustrates these safety features and their purpose.

Protector: It allows the Principal to designate a third party to monitor and record the Agent's actions. If the Principal has to resort to this level of oversight, this must be a last-resort option, with the Principal exhausting all other feasible options.

Article XII: Protector

SAFETY FEATURE: Implementing this option creates an administrative burden, but it also creates checks and balances. This option is a personal decision that the Principal must make for their future benefit.

	Place "Y" for Yes or "N" for No in the box and initial "✎" the line if the Principal desires the following:	**Restrict Agent's Powers by using a Protector**

"Y" or "N" Here ↑   Initial Here ↑

By designating "Y" for Yes, the Principal has enacted a Durable Protecting Power of Attorney (DPPOA). The role of the Protector is to safeguard the best interest and wishes of the Principal, primarily in a passive capacity, and to provide basic administrative support to the Agent. However, when the Agent violates their role as a Fiduciary, it is the role of the Protector to step in, relieve the Agent, and protect the Principal's rights and interests.

The date of DPPOA Execution: Month of: _____ Day of: _____ Year of: _____

A formal recording/filing (optional) of the POA is with the following:

Public Records:	Location:		Docket #	
	Address:		Page #	

The Principal designates the Protector (the first choice) with decision-making powers to adhere to the terms within the DPPOA.

Protector 1st choice →	Full Name:		
	Address:		
	Phone #:	Email:	
	Residence:	County:	State:

In the unlikely event that the Protector (the first choice) refuses, is unable, or is denied (by a Judge or Principal) to act as a Protector. The Principal designates the successor Protector (the second choice) with decision-making powers to adhere to the terms within the DPPOA.

Protector 2nd choice →	Full Name:		
	Address:		
	Phone #:	Email:	
	Residence:	County:	State:

In the unlikely event that the Protector (the second choice) refuses, is unable, or is denied (by a Judge or Principal) to act as a Protector. The Principal dictates that a court of legal jurisdiction shall appoint a Protector for the Principal with decision-making powers to adhere to the terms within the DPPOA.

A: An active Protector shall not serve as an acting Agent; this is to prevent a conflict of interest. The individual must either abstain or resign from one of the roles to perform the functions of the other.

B: The Protector (listed above) must be an Agent within the DPPOA to have power over the POA's Agents. The choice selection for Protector may not be in the same order as shown on the POA; if there is a conflict regarding choice selection designation, the POA shall take precedence.

Optional Safety Features

These documents come with **Optional Safety Features** to protect the Principal; the following example illustrates these safety features and explains why they exist.

Durability Provisions: This provision allows the Principal to "put in stone" per se the Agent's ability to continue to act on the Principal's behalf if the Principal were to suffer Incompetence, Incapacity, or Functioning Non-Socially in the future.

Article XIII: Durability Provisions

Statement of Understanding by the Principal: The Principal understands that the direction and choices implemented by the Agent as specified in this POA (if still active due to durability provision(s) and not previously revoked) shall continue, even if the Principal objects to the actions or decisions later when the Principal is functioning non-socially, incapacitated, or incompetent.

DIRECTIONS: The Principal must **place "Y"** for **Yes** in all applicable empty box spaces below and initial "🖊" on **the line** for activation of Durable Power(s). The Principal must **place "N"** for **No** to all applicable empty box spaces below **and initial "🖊" the line** for no activation of Durable Power(s). Durable Power(s) will not receive activation if the empty box space or the Principal's initial is void or left blank.

☐ "Y" or "N" Here ↑ Initial Here ↑	Place **"Y"** for **Yes** or **"N"** for **No** in the box and initial "🖊" the line if the Principal desires the following:	**(A)** Durability against Incompetence

DESCRIPTION: By designating **"Y"** for Yes, this POA shall continue if the Principal becomes incompetent; this POA shall survive the effects of incompetence and shall not be invalid, null, or void. Furthermore, the Agent's power and authority shall remain effective when the Principal is incompetent.

☐ "Y" or "N" Here ↑ Initial Here ↑	Place **"Y"** for **Yes** or **"N"** for **No** in the box and initial "🖊" the line if the Principal desires the following:	**(B)** Durability against Incapacity

DESCRIPTION: By designating **"Y"** for Yes, this POA shall continue if the Principal becomes incapacitated; this POA shall survive the effects of incapacity and shall not be invalid, null, or void. Furthermore, the Agent's power and authority shall remain effective when the Principal is incapacitated.

☐ "Y" or "N" Here ↑ Initial Here ↑	Place **"Y"** for **Yes** or **"N"** for **No** in the box and initial "🖊" the line if the Principal desires the following:	**(C)** Durability against Functioning Non-Socially

DESCRIPTION: By designating **"Y"** for Yes, this POA shall continue if the Principal functions Non-Socially; this POA shall survive the effects of functioning non-socially and shall not be invalid, null, or void. Furthermore, the Agent's power and authority shall remain effective when the Principal functions non-socially.

Recommendation:	The Agent should attach the **Affidavit of Principal's Health State** by a licensed Health Professional (dated before the expiration date) if the Principal is functioning non-socially, incapacitated, or incompetent when presenting the POA to any Third Party.

Optional Safety Features

These documents come with **Optional Safety Features** to protect the Principal; the following example illustrates these safety features and their purpose.

Require the Utilization of "Acknowledgment of Appointment by Agent": Require the Agent to sign off on the "Acknowledgment of Appointment by Agent" form before allowing the perspective Agent to act as the Principal's Agent. This would allow for greater accountability for the Agent's actions if litigation were to occur.

Article XVI: Acknowledgment of Appointment by the Agent

SAFETY FEATURE: Implementing this option creates an administrative burden, but it also creates checks and balances. This option is a personal decision that the Principal must make for their future benefit.

| | Place "Y" for Yes or "N" for No in the box and initial "✐" the line if the Principal desires the following: | Requires Utilization of Acknowledgment of Appointment by Agent Form |

"Y" or "N" Here ↑   Initial Here ↑

For brevity and consistency, the abbreviation of "**Acknowledgment of Appointment by Agent**" shall be "**Appointment.**" By designating "**Y**" for Yes, the Principal must fill out, sign, and notarize the Appointment as a condition of becoming the acting Agent. The Agent shall forfeit their right to serve as an Agent by default if the Agent fails to implement the Appointment. The successor Agent shall become the current acting Agent, provided the successor Agent executes the Appointment. The appointment shall become a prerequisite for the Agent to implement in all succession matters. If the Principal selects a Co-Power Sharing for Agents, implementing this Appointment shall still be a requirement for each Agent. When utilizing the POA with any Third Party, the Agent shall provide a copy of the Appointment to the Third Party. Failure to provide a copy of the Appointment to the Third Party shall result in the Third Party refusing and declining the POA.

Article XVIII: Authorization of Delegation of Agent's Power to another Agent

SAFETY FEATURE: Implementing this option creates an administrative burden, but it also creates checks and balances. This option is a personal decision that the Principal must make for their future benefit.

| | Place "Y" for Yes or "N" for No in the box and initial "✐" the line if the Principal desires the following: | Delegation of Agent's Powers to another Agent |

"Y" or "N" Here ↑   Initial Here ↑

By designating "**Y**" for Yes, the Principal allows delegating an Agent's powers to another Agent in **Article VII**. This discretionary power is useful when the acting Agent suffers inconveniences due to a lack of knowledge, logistics issues, or time constraints. The Agent who receives power from another Agent is the "Delegate." For transparency and record-keeping purposes, the utilization of the following forms shall occur: "**Delegation of Agent's Powers**" and "**Revocation of Delegate by (Agent, Principal, or Protector)**" with a copy mailed by the Agent to the Principal. If the Principal revokes an Agent, and the Agent has a Delegate, then the Delegate's powers are no longer active. If the Principal or Protector revokes an Agent due to a violation of Fiduciary duties, then that Agent shall not serve in the future as a Delegate. If the Principal or Protector revokes a Delegate for violating Fiduciary duties, then that Delegate shall not serve as an Agent forever.

Optional Safety Features

These documents come with **Optional Safety Features** to protect the Principal; the following example illustrates these safety features and their purpose.

Security Footer Setting: This ensures the document's legitimacy, thus making it extremely difficult to forge or tamper with this POA from interested parties.

Article XIX: Security Footer Setting

SAFETY FEATURE: To prevent fraud and ensure legitimacy, the Principal may desire to enact a security feature known as the **"Security Footer."** Security Footer is burdensome; however, if the Principal believes that a party will contest or illegitimately alter this POA, selecting the "High" setting may be desirable. The following pages will not usually have a security feature: (**01**) Cover Page, (**02**) Table of Contents, (**03**) Warning Page, (**04**) Informational Page, and (**05**) Intentionally blank separate page. The Principal requires the POA to have the following security setting: **Directions: Place a "✓" in the Security Level box.**

Security Level: ☐ None ☐ Low ☐ Moderate ☐ High

If the security selection is **"None,"** no initial on the Security Footer is required. If the security selection is **"Low,"** then the Principal's initial is required in the Security Footer. If the security selection is **"Moderate,"** then the Principal's and Notary's initials are required in the Security Footer. If the security selection is **"High,"** then the Principal's, Notary's, and Witness's initial is required in the Security Footer. The default option is "None" if the security selection is left blank (not "✓").

A: It might be suspicious if a page within this POA lacks the necessary initials, as stated in the Security Footer setting indicated above. In this event, the whole page shall be invalid and deemed unenforceable.

B: If a Witness but not the other Witness (when (**02**) two Witnesses are required) forgot to initial the Security Footer, but the Notary and Principal initial that page, then that page shall survive **Article XIX, Subsection A**. However, if no Notary's initial is present in the Security Footer and the Witness's initial is missing, then that page shall be subject to **Article XIX, Subsection A**.

C: Under State Law, if this POA is valid and enforceable with a Security Footer level of "Moderate," even though it is supposed to have a "High" Security Footer level." Then the following shall apply: If one or both Witnesses do not initial the Security Footer even though the Security Footer level is "High," then that page shall survive **Article XIX, Subsection A**, providing that the Principal and Notary have initialed the page.

D: If the Security Footer requires a Notary's Initial and the Notary's Initial is not present, the page shall be subject to **Article XIX, Subsection A**.

E: If the Security Footer requires a Principal's Initial and the Principal's Initial is not present, the page shall be subject to **Article XIX, Subsection A**.

F: If a Witness is also a potential Health Care Surrogate, Mental Health Care Surrogate, Agent, Guardian, or Conservator, then due to conflict of interest, the Witness shall not serve in such a fiduciary capacity unless the Witness gets approval through a court of competent jurisdiction to act in a fiduciary role.

G: To prevent fraud, every revocation requires a Notary Initial, Signature, and Seal; one or more Witnesses are not required.

This page is intentionally left blank

CHAPTER 03

Complex Limited Power of Attorney

CHAPTER 03

Overview

Complex Limited Power of Attorney

Overview

It is highly advantageous that the Principal trusts the person acting as their Agent completely for the Complex Limited Power of Attorney. That person shall have power over the Principal assets and affairs as if the Principal were there in person.

This Power of Attorney is "**Complex**" for the following reasons: (**01**) It names multiple Agents with successors Agent. (**02**) The effective date or expiration date may be contingent upon multiple variables. (**03**) There are springing, and sprinkling powers added. (**04**) Durable provisions are optional. (**05**) Multiple safety features are available; however, implementation is optional.

- ## Complex Limited Power of Attorney (CLPOA)　　(19 Pages Total)

  Only utilize this document if necessary and in a prudent manner. This Power of Attorney gives the Agent limed powers (written by the Principal) and ability regarding the Principal's property and affairs. **Please Note:** If the Principal requires a Power of Attorney that covers Banking, Financial, or General Activities, the Principal will probably be better off choosing the Complex Banking Power of Attorney, Complex Financial Power of Attorney, or Complex General Power of Attorney.

™

Complex Limited
Power of Attorney

Complex Limited Power of Attorney

Objective:

The objective of this Complex Limited Power of Attorney (CLPOA) is to give the individual whom the Principal has designated as the Agent limited power (written by the Principal) and ability regarding the Principal's property and affairs. This Power of Attorney is complex for the following reasons: (**01**) It names multiple Agents with the successor's Agent. (**02**) The effective or expiration date may be contingent upon multiple variables. (**03**) Springing and sprinkling powers were added. (**04**) Durable provision(s) are optional. (**05**) Multiple safety features are available; however, implementation is optional.

Do The Following:

Please note that the possibility exists that transactions or third parties may not permit using this CLPOA; suggest checking for unusual requirements or imposition in advance. The Principal should know that most financial institutions or businesses would only honor a durable power of attorney. Usually, vetting of the power of attorneys must occur first in the legal department before utilization due to liability reasons. Upon filling out the CLPOA, print off at least (**03**) three copies, (**01**) one for each of the following: Principal, Agent, and each financial institution or business. Please note that the possibility exists that financial institutions or businesses will only honor a power of attorney of their own making; thus, the Agent may have to sue to enforce a power of attorney. Other financial institutions or businesses may have policies requiring the account holder to provide a power of attorney in person for their "folder" before utilization. Most financial institutions or businesses will not accept a Non-Durable Power of Attorney.

Not A Court Order:

Please Note: This is not a court order. Executing this CLPOA is strictly voluntary. Implementing the CLPOA must be proactive to be effective and valid. It is highly advantageous that the Principal record/file (optional) the CLPOA with the courts or county clerk. Falsification of this CLPOA may constitute a criminal offense.

Note of Caution:

When filling out this CLPOA, please consider the following. The Purchaser or User should seek a legal professional's advice if the Purchaser or User is less than eighteen (18) years of age and currently deemed mentally incompetent or incapacitated. Feel free to utilize this CLPOA as a template. However, without legal representation in the situation above, this CLPOA would suffer litigation by Interested Third Parties and more than likely receive judgment as invalid. Remember, an active lawful court order covering the subject matter within this CLPOA will always take precedence if a conflict occurs. **Please Note:** If the Purchaser or User does have an active court order. The Purchaser or User can design this CLPOA, so it is not in conflict; however, seek the advice of a legal professional if there are any questions.

Complex Limited Power of Attorney

Table of Contents:

Helpful Suggestions / Recommendations:

- Most notaries who notarize a document for free as part of their occupation will usually only notarize one document versus having multiple originals. **Recommendation:** Find out what the Notary will do in advance.
- Keep the Original CLPOA in a safe place (preferably a fireproof vault or safe) and give an original copy to a trusted individual.
- Make multiple copies of this CLPOA. Give a copy to each interested Third Party. Maintain a list of who has copies of this CLPOA in their procession. Attach the list to the Original CLPOA in the Principal procession. If the CLPOA is revoked, refer to the list to retrieve the CLPOA in question.
- The easiest way to restrict this CLPOA is to establish an Expiration Date, preferably in five (**05**) to ten (**10**) year increments. Upon expiration of this CLPOA, the Principal will have to execute a new CLPOA to continue the agency relationship regarding the Principal's property and affairs.
- The Principal should execute an Affidavit of Principal's Health State by a licensed Health Professional if there are questions or doubts regarding the Principal's capacity, competence, or social functionality. Attach the executed Affidavit of Principal's Health State to the Original CLPOA. If applicable, give a trusted individual an original copy of the Affidavit of Principal's Health State.

Complex Limited Power of Attorney

Important Document

- Before signing this Complex Limited Power of Attorney (CLPOA), the Principal should know these important facts. This CLPOA aims to give the individual the Principal designates as their "Agent" **the limited power (written by the Principal) and ability regarding the Principal's property and affairs.**

- **Please Note:** While the Principal is competent, the Principal still has all the power and rights to control their property and affairs as the Principal deems fit, despite any powers the Principal may have bestowed.

- The Principal must talk to their Agent often, specifically about what the Agent does while using this CLPOA. If the Agent is not following the Principal's written instructions, the Principal may revoke this CLPOA or end the Agent's powers.

- **Beware:** Please note that the possibility exists that Third Parties or certain transactions may not permit the use of this CLPOA; it is advisable to check in advance, if possible, for any special requirements or imposition.

- This CLPOA does not impose a duty on the Agent to exercise discretionary powers. However, when using these powers, the Agent must use due care to act for the Principal's benefit and adhere to this CLPOA. The Agent must act consistently with the Principal's desires, as stated in the CLPOA. Unless the Principal says or limits otherwise, the Agent has the same level of authority to make decisions. **Please Note:** A court could take away the powers of an Agent if the Agent authorizes anything that is illegal or acts contrary to this CLPOA.

- The Agent may exercise these powers throughout the Principal's lifetime unless otherwise limited in writing (time duration or event occurrence). Furthermore, these powers will continue to exist and shall be enforceable (if the durable provision(s) are active) if the Principal develops one or more of the following: **(01)** have a disability that renders the Principal to function non-socially. **(02)** The Principal is incapacitated. **(03)** The Principal is incompetent.

- This CLPOA does not authorize anyone to make health care decisions for the Principal. The Principal should implement the following if the Principal wishes to have health care decisions made: **(01)** Advanced Medical Health Directive, **(02)** Advanced Mental Health Directive, **(03)** Do Not Resuscitate Advance Directive (DNR), **(04)** Durable Power of Attorney for Health Care, **(05)** Declaration of Health Care (Living Will) and **(06)** Declaration of Organs & Tissues Donation (Anatomical Gifts).

- This CLPOA does not authorize anyone to decide guardianship regarding a minor or a disabled adult; neither gives the Agent the right to delegate Parental or Guardian authority. The Principal should implement the following if the Principal wishes to delegate their Parental / Guardian authority: **(01)** Simple or Complex Limited Power of Attorney for Minor Child. **(02)** Durable Power of Attorney for Health Care of Minor Child. **(03)** Declaration of Guardianship & Conservatorship for Minor Child. **(04)** Declaration of Guardianship & Conservatorship for the Disabled.

- This CLPOA does not authorize anyone to decide guardianship or conservatorship regarding the Principal, nor does it give the Agent's powers of delegation regarding the Guardian or Conservator authority. If the Principal wishes to establish a Guardian or Conservator, the Principal should implement the following: **(01)** Declaration of Guardianship & Conservatorship.

- The creation and design of this CLPOA require no legal assistance to complete. The Principal or Agent should seek advice from a licensed Attorney for clarification or questions regarding this CLPOA.

- The Principal may revoke this CLPOA if the Principal is competent. The Principal should contact a licensed Attorney if the Agent continues to act after the Principal has revoked the Agent's powers and notified the Agent of their termination. Should the Principal revoke the Agent's authority, a written Revocation should be hand-delivered or mailed to where this CLPOA has been utilized.

- Use this CLPOA only after careful consideration. The Principals' execution and implementation of this CLPOA should be free from pressure. Do not name an Agent or grant power unless it is the Principal's choice.

© 2018 by Paul M. Paquette; Form v3.00
All Rights Reserved; Paquette Publications

Complex Limited
Power of Attorney

You must verify the Agent's identity
with a government-issued picture I.D.

Page 01 of 16

Complex Limited Power of Attorney

Article I: Creation Statement

The Principal (stated below) revokes every previous Complex Limited Power of Attorney with an execution date predating this document.

Principal →

Full Name:	
Address:	
Phone #:	**Email:**
Residence:	**County:** **State:**

The Principal affirms the following in the Witnesses and Notary presence: **(01)** The Principal is at least eighteen **(18)** years or older. **(02)** The Principal is of sound and disposing mind (emotionally and mentally competent) to make or request this Complex Limited Power of Attorney. **(03)** The Principal has the capacity with full memory or necessary mental faculties to understand and comprehend these actions. **(04)** The Principal willfully and voluntarily executes this Complex Limited Power of Attorney. The following abbreviations shall be used for brevity and consistency: Complex Limited Power of Attorney shall be "**CLPOA**," and Attorney-In-Fact shall be "**Agent**."

Article II: Purpose

As stated in **Article VII**, The Principal appoints, authorizes, and designates the following Agent to make decisions and perform actions for the Principal according to the CLPOA terms and conditions as indicated in **Article III** through **Article XX**.

Article III: Effective Date of CLPOA

The Principal wants the following regarding the effective date for the legal enforcement of this CLPOA: The Principal can choose from **(02)** two options; however, **options A** and **B** are mutually exclusive. **Option A** shall be the default option in the event of ambiguities.

"Y" or "N" Here ↑   Initial Here ↑

Place "**Y**" for Yes or "**N**" for No in the box and initial "✐" the line if the Principal desires the following:

(A) Effective Immediately

By designating "**Y**" for Yes, the effective date of this CLPOA shall begin from the day of execution, as stated in **Article XX**. If durability provision(s) are active in **Article XIII**, those provision(s) shall immediately take effect.

"Y" or "N" Here ↑   Initial Here ↑

Place "**Y**" for Yes or "**N**" for No in the box and initial "✐" the line if the Principal desires the following:

(B) Effective if Events are Trigger

By designating "**Y**" for Yes, the effective date of this CLPOA shall begin when such events transpire or occur, as outlined in **Article V**: "**Springing Powers**." If durability provision(s) are active in **Article XIII**, the durability provision(s) shall be active when such events transpire, as outlined in **Article V**: "**Springing Powers**."

Article IV: Expiration Date of CLPOA

The Principal wants the following regarding the expiration date for the legal enforcement of this CLPOA: The Principal can choose from **(02)** two options; however, **options A** and **B** are mutually exclusive. **Option B** shall be the default option in the event of ambiguities.

"Y" or "N" Here ↑   Initial Here ↑

Place "**Y**" for Yes or "**N**" for No in the box and initial "✐" the line if the Principal desires the following:

(A) Expire by a Define Date

By designating "**Y**" for Yes, the Principal wants to establish an expiration date for this CLPOA as stated below.

The date that CLPOA Expires: Month of: _____   Day of: _____   Year of: _____

1ˢᵗ Witness: _____   2ⁿᵈ Witness: _____   Notary Public: _____   Principal: _____

© 2018 by Paul M. Paquette; Form v3.00
All Rights Reserved; Paquette Publications

Complex Limited
Power of Attorney

You must verify the Agent's identity
with a government-issued picture I.D.

Page 02 of 16

Place "Y" for Yes or "N" for No in the box and initial "🖊" the line if the Principal desires the following:

(B)

Expire by Revocation

"Y" or "N" Here ↑   Initial Here ↑

By designating "Y" for Yes, the expiration date of this CLPOA shall end when the Principal revokes this CLPOA while in a Healthy state or other methods as outlined in **Article XI Subsection B.**

Article V: Springing Powers

SAFETY FEATURE: By implementing this option, the Principal creates an administrative burden but also creates checks and balances. This option is a personal decision that the Principal must determine for their future benefit. **STATEMENT OF ACKNOWLEDGMENT:** The Principal acknowledges and states that springing powers shall only occur if **Article III Option B** is active. Furthermore, the Principal dictates that one of the following scenarios below (if selected) shall transpire/occur to activate the Springing Powers of this CLPOA.

DIRECTIONS: The Principal must **place "Y"** for **Yes** in all applicable empty box spaces below and initial "🖊" on **the line** for activation of Springing Power(s). The Principal must **place "N"** for **No** to all applicable empty box spaces below **and initial "🖊" the line** for no activation of Springing Power(s). Springing Power(s) will not receive activation if the empty box space or the Principal's initial is void or left blank.

"Y" or "N" Here ↑   Initial Here ↑

Incapacitation

The Principal health state is **Incapacitation**; read **Article VI Subsection A**.

"Y" or "N" Here ↑   Initial Here ↑

Incompetent

The Principal health state is **Incompetent**; read **Article VI Subsection B** for more details.

"Y" or "N" Here ↑   Initial Here ↑

Function Non-Socially

The Principal health state is **Function Non-Socially**; read **Article VI Subsection C** for more details.

"Y" or "N" Here ↑   Initial Here ↑

Active Duty – Overseas or Abroad

The Principal is on **Active Duty either overseas or abroad** for a duration that lasts longer than **(07)** seven days (proof will consist of military orders or a signed, preferably notarized, letter from the Principal).

"Y" or "N" Here ↑   Initial Here ↑

Business Trip – Overseas or Abroad

The Principal is on a **business trip either overseas or abroad** for a duration that lasts longer than **(07)** seven days (proof will consist of a copy of the ticket purchased or a signed, preferably notarized, letter from the Principal).

"Y" or "N" Here ↑   Initial Here ↑

Incarcerated in Jail, Prison, Correctional Facilities

The Principal is in **jail, prison, or any other correctional facility** where freedom of personal movement is reduced or denied (proof will consist of evidence of incarceration or a signed, preferably notarized, letter from the Principal).

"Y" or "N" Here ↑   Initial Here ↑

Recognize as being Officially Missing

The Principal is officially missing (proof will consist of the missing person report by the government or law enforcement authority).

"Y" or "N" Here ↑   Initial Here ↑

1ˢᵗ Witness: _____   2ⁿᵈ Witness: _____   Notary Public: _____   Principal: _____

© 2018 by Paul M. Paquette; Form v3.00
All Rights Reserved; Paquette Publications

Complex Limited
Power of Attorney

You must verify the Agent's identity
with a government-issued picture I.D.

Page 03 of 16

Homestead is uninhabitable or lost

"Y" or "N" Here ↑   Initial Here ↑

The Principal **Homestead is uninhabitable or lost** due to a natural disaster or other causes (proof will consist of one or more of the following: an insurance report or estimate, an inspector's report, or a report by a government or law enforcement authority).

Medical or Mental Health Institution / Facility

"Y" or "N" Here ↑   Initial Here ↑

The Principal has been in the custodial care of a Medical or Mental Health Institution/Facility for more than (**07**) seven days (proof will consist of evidence of stay at a Mental Health Institution/Facility or a signed, preferably notarized, letter from the Principal).

Kidnapped, held for ransom, sold into slavery, serfdom, sexual servitude, or unfree labor

"Y" or "N" Here ↑   Initial Here ↑

The Principal is **kidnapped, held for ransom, sold into slavery, serfdom, sexual servitude, or unfree labor** (proof will consist of a statement or report by the government or law enforcement authority or a verifiable and credible ransom demand or ransom letter).

Article VI: Health Status Definitions

A: Incapacitation shall occur if a court of competent jurisdiction has issued a court order stating that the Principal is incapacitated. Alternatively, the Principal currently has a medical and mental health condition diagnosed by (**02**) two licensed independent Physicians who have personally examined the Principal. Under the penalty of perjury, the Physicians stated in writing that the Principal demonstrates one or more of the following conditions. (**01**) The Principal cannot make, participate, or communicate a decision regarding their health care. (**02**) The Principal cannot manage the following: their care, property, or financial affairs. When trying to conceptualize what an incapacitated individual can do, think of an individual unable to control their motor movement and needing help to do regular tasks. Examples include (but are not limited to) the following: Amyotrophic Lateral Sclerosis (ALS), Primary Lateral Sclerosis (PLS), Progressive Bulbar Palsy (PBP), Progressive Muscular Atrophy (PMA), Pseudobulbar Palsy, and Parkinson's disease.

B: Incompetent shall occur if a court of competent jurisdiction has issued a court order stating that the Principal is incompetent. Alternatively, the Principal currently has a medical and mental health condition with diagnosis by (**02**) two independent Licensed Health Professionals (any combination will do) that serve in the following capacity (Physician, Clinical Psychologist, or Psychiatrist) who has personally examined the Principal. In writing, the Health Professionals state that the Principal demonstrates one or more of the following under the penalty of perjury. (**01**) The Principal cannot understand and appreciate the extent, nature, and probable consequences of a proposed medical and mental health decision that may or may not have life-sustaining implications. (**02**) The Principal cannot make an informed, intelligent decision in a reasonable amount of time. (**03**) The Principal cannot communicate a coherent decision no matter how simple the communication process is. (**04**) The Principal cannot rationally evaluate the risks and benefits of a proposed medical and mental health decision compared to the risks and benefits of alternatives. Examples include (but are not limited to) the following: Alzheimer's disease, Huntington's disease, Schizophrenia, Psychotic Disorder, and Severe Dementia. **Please Note:** An individual with a mental illness, advanced age, or developmental disability does not automatically imply or constitute a lack of decisional capacity.

C: Function Non-Socially shall occur if a court of competent jurisdiction has issued a court order stating that the Principal is functioning non-socially. Alternatively, the Principal currently has a medical and mental health condition diagnosed by (**02**) two licensed independent Physicians who have personally examined the Principal. The Physicians stated in writing, under the penalty of perjury, that the Principal cannot demonstrate one or more of the following: to recognize people, communicate with people, and interact with people in a meaningful way.

D: By the term **Healthy**, the Principal means the following: exhibit capacity with complete mental competence, thus fully capable of independent thought and actions, and function socially.

1st Witness: _____   2nd Witness: _____   Notary Public: _____   Principal: _____

Article VII: Designation of Agent

The Principal should only designate an Agent if that individual is **Reliable**, **Trustworthy**, and **Competent** to manage the Principal's affairs. For legal reasons, all Agents must be competent and at least eighteen (**18**) years or older. None of the following individuals (non-relative) may serve as the Principal's Agent. (**A**) Any individual who serves as an Owner, Operator, or employee of a Health Care Facility (Medical, Mental, or Assisted Living) in which the Principal is currently a Patient / Client unless the employee serves solely as a Notary Public. (**B**) Any individual who serves as an Owner, Operator, or employee of a Final Dispositional Facility (Funerary Home, Crematory Authority, and Cemetery Authority) unless the employee serves solely as a Notary Public. (**C**) Any Doctor, Physician, Psychologist, Psychiatrist, Social Worker, Financial Advisor, or Financial Manager in which the Principal is currently a Patient / Client. Automatic Revocation of the Spouse designation as Agent shall occur if the following happens: (**01**) Dissolution or annulment of the marriage. (**02**) Proceedings are currently active for Dissolution of Marriage. (**03**) The Principal currently lives in a separate physical location from their Spouse for more than (**02**) two months with the intention of a divorce. The Principal designates the following individual as the Agent, the first choice, with decision-making powers in adherence to the terms and conditions specified in this CLPOA.

AGENT 1st choice →

Full Name:	
Address:	
Phone #:	Email:
Residence:	County:	State:

In the unlikely event that the Agent (the first choice) refuses, is unable, or is denied (by a Judge or Principal) to act as an Agent. The Principal designates the successor Agent (the second choice) with decision-making powers to adhere to the terms and conditions specified in this CLPOA.

AGENT 2nd choice →

Full Name:	
Address:	
Phone #:	Email:
Residence:	County:	State:

In the unlikely event that the Agent (the second choice) refuses, is unable, or is denied (by a Judge or Principal) to act as an Agent. The Principal designates the successor Agent (the third choice) with decision-making powers to adhere to the terms and conditions specified in this CLPOA.

AGENT 3rd Choice →

Full Name:	
Address:	
Phone #:	Email:
Residence:	County:	State:

In the unlikely event that the Agent (the third choice) refuses, is unable, or is denied (by a Judge or Principal) to act as an Agent. The Principal designates the successor Agent (the fourth choice) with decision-making powers to adhere to the terms and conditions specified in this CLPOA.

AGENT 4th Choice →

Full Name:	
Address:	
Phone #:	Email:
Residence:	County:	State:

In the unlikely event that the Agent (the fourth choice) refuses, is unable, or is denied (by a Judge or Principal) to act as an Agent. The Principal designates the successor Agent (the fifth choice) with decision-making powers to adhere to the terms and conditions specified in this CLPOA.

AGENT 5th Choice →

Full Name:	
Address:	
Phone #:	Email:
Residence:	County:	State:

In the unlikely event that the Agent (the fifth choice) refuses, is unable, or is denied (by a Judge or Principal) to act as an Agent. The Principal dictates that a court of legal jurisdiction shall appoint an Agent for the Principal to act in adherence to the terms of the CLPOA.

1st Witness: _____   2nd Witness: _____   Notary Public: _____   Principal: _____

Article VIII: Agent Co-Power Sharing

SAFETY FEATURE: Implementing this option creates an administrative burden, but it also creates checks and balances. This option is a personal decision that the Principal must make for their future benefit.

"Y" or "N" Here ↑ Initial Here ↑	Place **"Y"** for Yes or **"N"** for No in the box and initial "✐" the line if the Principal desires the following:

Enable Agent Co-Power Sharing

By designating **"Y"** for Yes, the Principal has enabled co-power sharing for the Agent(s), which shall initially be the first and second choice Agent. The Agent(s) shall have the authority and power to make joint decisions on the Principal's behalf in a co-power-sharing arrangement. Co-power sharing involves the Agent(s) making and implementing decisions together. Every joint decision must be in writing, with both Agents approving such decisions by signature. Succession for co-power sharing shall occur when an Agent is either unable or unwilling to accept or continue the appointment as the Agent; thus, the third choice as Agent shall take the place of the departing Agent. The succession for Agent shall continue in the manner above (as illustrated when the third choice for Agent assumes powers) until every named Agent is unable or unwilling to accept or continue the appointment as Agent. Furthermore, the Agents agree to perform all their duties as follows:

A: The Agents shall collaborate and share all knowledge and activities via letter, text, phone, or email. Email is the preferred method of communication.

B: The Agents shall not change the following: Account Information, Security Questions, Log-In Screen Name or I.D., and Passwords without having both active Agents agree to such changes in advance (preferably in writing email). An Agent shall be relieved of their powers/duties if an Agent initiates such changes to prevent the other Agent from knowing what activities are occurring.

C: Transparency is paramount, thus requiring continuous active support among all Agent(s). Disclosure of account status or changes must occur to all Agents within (07) seven days before activation or deactivation. Furthermore, all account information, security settings, and password information shall be up-to-date and continuously dispersed to all Agents (active) as soon as possible via the most efficient means of communication.

D: All Agents are accountable for their actions and shall not act alone without consent or prior agreement from the other Co-Agent; failure to do so may result in criminal or civil proceedings.

Resignation:	The Agent may resign by notifying the Principal, Protector (Complex & Durable POA), Co-Agent, Successor Agent, or the Principal's Guardian. The resignation must be in writing by certified mail, statutory overnight delivery (return receipt requested), or email.

Article IX: Powers, Rights, Privileges

Statement from the Principal to the Third Parties: All Third Parties dealing in good faith with the Agent may fully rely upon the Agent's power and authority to act on the Principal's behalf and in the Principal's name. All Third Parties may accept and rely on agreements and other instruments entered or executed by the Agent under this CLPOA.

Power and Authority to Acts: The Agent's powers include the ability to act in the Principal name, place, and stead in any way (in parts or whole) that is proper and prudent. The Agent's powers include acting to the fullest and greatest extent possible in which the Principal is permissible by law to act through an Agent with the Principal's best interest and welfare in mind.

The Agent's Powers: The Agent shall have the full power and authority to exercise, perform, manage, and conduct in a fiduciary capacity and shall act with utmost good faith, fair dealing, full disclosure, and fidelity towards the Principal. The Agent shall have any incidental rights required to conduct and perform the specific powers granted herein. The Agent shall exercise the Principal legal rights and powers, including those rights and powers that the Principal may acquire in the future.

DIRECTIONS: The Principal must **place "Y"** for **Yes** in all applicable empty box spaces below and initial "✐" on **the line** for activation of Agent's Power(s). The Principal must **place "N"** for **No** to all applicable empty box spaces below **and initial "✐" the line** for no activation of Agent's Power(s). Agent's Power(s) will not receive activation if the empty box space or the Principal's initial is void or left blank.

1ˢᵗ Witness: _____   **2ⁿᵈ Witness:** _____   **Notary Public:** _____   **Principal:** _____

Complex Limited
Power of Attorney

You must verify the Agent's identity
with a government-issued picture I.D.

Page 06 of 16

Place "Y" for Yes or "N" for No in the box and initial "✐" the line if the Principal desires the following:

(A)

"Y" or "N" Here ↑   Initial Here ↑   Preferably Type or Legible Writing in Ink for the Description into the above space ↑

DESCRIPTION: By designating "Y" for Yes, the Agent's powers include the ability to do the following:

Specify in Detail

Preferably Type or Legible Writing in Ink

Place "Y" for Yes or "N" for No in the box and initial "✐" the line if the Principal desires the following:

(B)

"Y" or "N" Here ↑   Initial Here ↑   Preferably Type or Legible Writing in Ink for the Description into the above space ↑

DESCRIPTION: By designating "Y" for Yes, the Agent's powers include the ability to do the following:

Specify in Detail

Preferably Type or Legible Writing in Ink

Place "Y" for Yes or "N" for No in the box and initial "✐" the line if the Principal desires the following:

(C)

"Y" or "N" Here ↑   Initial Here ↑   Preferably Type or Legible Writing in Ink for the Description into the above space ↑

DESCRIPTION: By designating "Y" for Yes, the Agent's powers include the ability to do the following:

Specify in Detail

Preferably Type or Legible Writing in Ink

Place "Y" for Yes or "N" for No in the box and initial "✐" the line if the Principal desires the following:

(D)

"Y" or "N" Here ↑   Initial Here ↑   Preferably Type or Legible Writing in Ink for the Description into the above space ↑

DESCRIPTION: By designating "Y" for Yes, the Agent's powers include the ability to do the following:

Specify in Detail

Preferably Type or Legible Writing in Ink

1st Witness: _____   2nd Witness: _____   Notary Public: _____   Principal: _____

Place "Y" for Yes or "N" for No in the box and initial "✐" the line if the Principal desires the following:

(E)

"Y" or "N" Here ↑   Initial Here ↑   Preferably Type or **Legible Writing in Ink for the Description into the above space ↑**

DESCRIPTION: By designating "Y" for Yes, the Agent's powers include the ability to do the following:

Specify in Detail   Preferably Type or Legible Writing in Ink

Place "Y" for Yes or "N" for No in the box and initial "✐" the line if the Principal desires the following:

(F) Other Terms: (Conditions, Prohibitions, Restriction, Exceptions, Additions, Limitation, Extensions, and Special Rules)

"Y" or "N" Here ↑   Initial Here ↑

DESCRIPTION: By designating "Y" for Yes, the Agent's powers may be subject to the following regarding **Other Terms**: conditions, prohibitions, restrictions, exceptions, additions, limitations, extensions, or any special rules as typed in the box below. If there are any contradictions concerning **Article IX Subsections A through E**, the Principal shall type a brief explanation for the contradiction.

Specify in Detail   Preferably Type or Legible writing in Ink

Article X: Restrictions on Agent's Powers

Regardless of what authorization or powers bestow in **Article IX Subsection A through E,** the Agent shall not do or perform the following: **(01)** The Agent shall not make a loan to oneself, another name Agent, or a beneficiary of the Agent. **(02)** The Agent shall not take a service fee as an Agent. **(03)** The Agent shall not create, modify, or revoke a trust. **(04)** The Agent shall not use the Principal's property to fund a trust for someone other than the Principal or a trust that does not benefit the Principal greater than seventy (70%) percent. **(05)** The Agent shall not create or change a Beneficiary's interest in the Principal's property. **(06)** The Agent shall not create or change the Principal's interest in the Principal's property solely for the benefit of another. **(07)** The Agent shall not designate or change the designation of beneficiaries to receive any property, benefit, or contract right on the Principal's death. **(08)** The Agent shall not make or revoke a gift of the Principal property in trust or another arrangement. **(09)** The Agent shall not make or revoke a gift on the Principal's behalf. **(10)** The Agent shall not exercise any powers that would cause the Principal's assets to become taxable to the Agent or the Agent's estate for any income, estate, or inheritance tax. **(11)** The Agent shall not forgive debts owed to the Principal, disclaim, or waive benefits payable to the Principal. **(12)** The Agent shall not execute, publish, declare, amend, or revoke the following: last will, codicil, or any will substitute on the Principal's behalf. **(13)** The Agent shall not perform duties under a contract that requires the Principal's services. **(14)** The Agent shall not make an affidavit about the Principal's knowledge that is unknown to the Agent personally. **(15)** The Agent shall not vote in any governmental public election on behalf of the Principal unless the Agent has a notarized letter stating who the Principal's candidates and voting preferences are regarding that public election. **(16)** The Agent shall not exercise powers and authority granted to the Principal as Trustee or a court-appointed Fiduciary. **(17)** The Agent shall not exercise the right to make a disclaimer on behalf of the Principal, except for a disclaimer of a detrimental transfer or acceptance made with the court's approval. **(18)** The Agent shall not enjoin (add or transfer) ownership or title to the Principal's funds or assets in the Agent's name alone. **Please Note:** Waiver of these restrictions shall only occur if the Principal grants written permission in **Article IX Subsection F.**

1ˢᵗ Witness: _____   **2ⁿᵈ Witness:** _____   **Notary Public:** _____   **Principal:** _____

Article XI: Revocation

A: The Principal may revoke the CLPOA in writing for any reason without prior notice to the Agent or any Third Parties. However, in part(s) or whole, any Revocation shall require a Notary Public attesting to the revocation to ensure the authenticity and legitimacy of the Principal's actions.

B: Revocation Methods: Revocation of this CLPOA shall only occur in part(s) or whole by the following methods: **(01)** A new CLPOA that states all prior CLPOAs are revoked in writing. **(02)** The Principal revokes the CLPOA in a formal (type) manner with the Principal's signature and notarization. **(03)** The Principal willfully destroys all original (sign and seal) CLPOA and requests the destruction of all copies in writing. **(04)** The appropriate authorities have declared the death of the Principal. **(05)** A court of competent jurisdiction has issued a court order to terminate the Principal's CLPOA, in parts or whole.

C: All other Revocation methods shall be invalid and unenforceable, even if they are legally allowable.

Article XII: Protector

SAFETY FEATURE: Implementing this option creates an administrative burden, but it also creates checks and balances. This option is a personal decision that the Principal must make for their future benefit.

Place "Y" for Yes or "N" for No in the box and initial "✎" the line if the Principal desires the following:

Restrict Agent's Powers by using a Protector

"Y" or "N" Here ↑   Initial Here ↑

By designating "Y" for Yes, the Principal has enacted a Durable Protecting Power of Attorney (DPPOA). The role of the Protector is to safeguard the best interest and wishes of the Principal, primarily in a passive capacity, and to provide basic administrative support to the Agent. However, when the Agent violates their role as a Fiduciary, it is the role of the Protector to step in, relieve the Agent, and protect the Principal's rights and interests.

The date of DPPOA Execution: Month of: _____   Day of: _____   Year of: _____

A formal recording/filing (optional) of the DPPOA is with the following:

| **Public Records:** | Location: | | Docket # | |
| | Address: | | Page # | |

The Principal designates the Protector (the first choice) with decision-making powers to adhere to the terms within the DPPOA.

Protector 1st choice →	Full Name:	
	Address:	
	Phone #:	Email:
	Residence:	County:	State:

In the unlikely event that the Protector (the first choice) refuses, is unable, or is denied (by a Judge or Principal) to act as a Protector. The Principal designates the successor Protector (the second choice) with decision-making powers to adhere to the terms within the DPPOA.

Protector 2nd choice →	Full Name:	
	Address:	
	Phone #:	Email:
	Residence:	County:	State:

In the unlikely event that the Protector (the second choice) refuses, is unable, or is denied (by a Judge or Principal) to act as a Protector. The Principal dictates that a court of legal jurisdiction shall appoint a Protector for the Principal with decision-making powers to adhere to the terms within the DPPOA.

A: An active Protector shall not serve as an acting Agent; this is to prevent a conflict of interest. The individual must either abstain or resign from one of the roles to perform the functions of the other.

B: The Protector (listed above) must be an Agent within the DPPOA to have power over the CLPOA's Agents. The choice selection for Protector may not be in the same order as shown on the CLPOA; if there is a conflict regarding choice selection designation, the CLPOA shall take precedence.

1st Witness: _____   2nd Witness: _____   Notary Public: _____   Principal: _____

Article XIII: Durability Provisions

Statement of Understanding by the Principal: The Principal understands that the direction and choices implemented by the Agent as specified in this CLPOA (if still active due to durability provision(s) and not previously revoked) shall continue, even if the Principal objects to the actions or decisions later when the Principal is functioning non-socially, incapacitated, or incompetent.

DIRECTIONS: The Principal must **place "Y"** for **Yes** in all applicable empty box spaces below and initial "✎" on **the line** for activation of Durable Power(s). The Principal must **place "N"** for **No** to all applicable empty box spaces below **and initial "✎" the line** for no activation of Durable Power(s). Durable Power(s) will not receive activation if the empty box space or the Principal's initial is void or left blank.

"Y" or "N" Here ↑   Initial Here ↑   Place "Y" for Yes or "N" for No in the box and initial "✎" the line if the Principal desires the following: **(A)**   **Durability against Incompetence**

DESCRIPTION: By designating "Y" for Yes, this CLPOA shall continue if the Principal becomes incompetent; this CLPOA shall survive the effects of incompetence and shall not be invalid, null, or void. Furthermore, the Agent's power and authority shall remain effective when the Principal is incompetent.

"Y" or "N" Here ↑   Initial Here ↑   Place "Y" for Yes or "N" for No in the box and initial "✎" the line if the Principal desires the following: **(B)**   **Durability against Incapacity**

DESCRIPTION: By designating "Y" for Yes, this CLPOA shall continue if the Principal becomes incapacitated; this CLPOA shall survive the effects of incapacity and shall not be invalid, null, or void. Furthermore, the Agent's power and authority shall remain effective when the Principal is incapacitated.

"Y" or "N" Here ↑   Initial Here ↑   Place "Y" for Yes or "N" for No in the box and initial "✎" the line if the Principal desires the following: **(C)**   **Durability against Functioning Non-Socially**

DESCRIPTION: By designating "Y" for Yes, this CLPOA shall continue if the Principal functions Non-Socially; this CLPOA shall survive the effects of functioning non-socially and shall not be invalid, null, or void. Furthermore, the Agent's power and authority shall remain effective when the Principal functions non-socially.

Recommendation: The Agent should attach the **Affidavit of Principal's Health State** by a licensed Health Professional (dated before the expiration date) if the Principal is functioning non-socially, incapacitated, or incompetent when presenting the CLPOA to any Third Party.

Article XIV: Additional Legal Provisions

A: Reliance by Third Parties: To induce any Third Party to act, the Principal agrees that any Third Party receiving a duly executed copy/facsimile of this CLPOA may act upon hereunder. The revocation shall be ineffective until the Third Party receives notice or knowledge of the revocation. The Principal, Principal's heir(s), executor(s), administrator(s), legal or personal representative(s), and assign(s) agree to indemnify and hold harmless to the Third Party from and against all claims due to relying upon this CLPOA.

B: Notice to Third Party: A Third Party who fails to honor a properly executed CLPOA may be liable to the Principal, the Agent, the Principal's heirs, assigns, or estate. Liabilities may include (but are not limited to) the following: civil penalty plus damages, costs, and fees associated with the failure to comply with the CLPOA.

C: Compensation: Any individual serving in a fiduciary capacity in adherence to this CLPOA shall not receive compensation for the performance of their authority, rights, and responsibilities. However, the Fiduciary may receive reimbursement (if possible) for reasonable and necessary expenses incurred in performing their authority, rights, and responsibilities. If the Principal wishes to compensate the Agent, the Principal shall specify in detail in **Article IX Subsection F**.

D: Binding on Successors: This CLPOA and all its provisions shall become effective upon execution. All provisions shall be binding upon the heir(s), executor(s), administrator(s), legal or personal representative(s), and assign(s) and all fiduciaries' successors of the Principal as fully allowable by law.

1ˢᵗ Witness: _____   2ⁿᵈ Witness: _____   Notary Public: _____   Principal: _____

E: Original Counterparts: If multiple originals of this CLPOA have been executed, each such counterpart original shall have equal force and effect. Any photocopy of this CLPOA shall have the same force and effect as the original. **Suggestion:** Shade the Notary Public Seal when making a photocopy of CLPOA.

F: Surety or Bond: No individual named as an approved Agent selected for consideration by a Judge shall require the filing or furnishing of a bond, surety, or other security in any jurisdiction. If, despite this CLPOA, a bond is necessary, the Principal requests that it be without sureties and in a nominal amount.

G: Indemnification of Fiduciary: No individual serving within a fiduciary capacity named in this CLPOA shall incur any liability by the Principal for acting or refraining from acting under this CLPOA except in instances of the Fiduciary's negligence or wanton, willful, or reckless misconduct.

H: Indemnification of Third Parties: Third Parties that act in good faith, based on this CLPOA, shall not be subject to liability (criminal or civil) or professional disciplinary action for such reliance, except for the Third Parties' negligence or wanton, willful, or reckless misconduct.

I: Recordation: Recording this CLPOA with the county auditor, recording officer, et cetera is permissible, provided it serves a practical legal purpose or reason.

J: Relative Conflict: If the approved Agent selected for consideration by a Judge is a Spouse or is an Adult Child/Ward of the Principal. The Principal waives any conflict of interest that their Spouse or Adult Child/Ward might have due to potential inheritance or beneficiary arrangements.

K: Definition of Child/Ward: As used in this CLPOA, "Child" shall include any individual the Principal legally adopts. The term "Ward" shall consist of any individual legally in the Principal's care who is also the acting Guardian.

L: Fiduciaries: The term Fiduciaries shall include the following: Agent, Medical Health Care Surrogate, Mental Health Care Surrogate, Guardian, or Conservator. Be aware that the Principal reserves the right to designate or nominate other individuals as Fiduciaries in other legal documents to act on the Principal's behalf.

M: Transfer of Fiduciary Powers: No Agent shall have the rights or powers to any acts, power, duty, right, or obligation relating to any person, matter, transaction, or property in which the Principal is serving as a Fiduciary (Trustee, custodian, or personal representative) for someone else.

N: Modification: Upon execution, changes to this CLPOA shall not occur. If the Principal wants to change this CLPOA, the Principal must make an entirely new one. However, revocation of any part(s) of this CLPOA may occur if it is in writing; once a part(s) receives revocation, it shall be permanent. Alterations (strikes out, cross out, and blackouts) of any provisions or writing within this CLPOA shall have no bearing in a court of law and shall remain active and valid as to their original intent.

O: Picture I.D.: The Principal requires verifying the Agent's identity with a government-issued picture ID. The Principal does not require it to be current and up to date; all that the Principal requires is the ability to confirm their facial features in a picture from an official governmental source.

P: Delegation: The Agent shall not delegate their power or rights to individuals unless **Article XVII (Authorization of Delegation of Agent's Power to another Agent)** is active.

Q: Durability: If one or more of the durability provisions in **Article XIII** is active and applicable, then this CLPOA shall remain viable and legally enforceable unless the Principal, while in a Healthy State, implements a Revocation in adherence to **Article XI Subsection B.**

R: Conflicting Provisions: If one or more provisions conflict due to the scope and nature of the powers given, the Fiduciary powers shall be reduced in the provision or a subset thereof that is more conservative and prudent in scope and nature.

S: Headings (Article & Subsection): Article and Subsection Headings in Bold Face are for informational purposes only and serve as a guide to what the subject entails. However, the heading may not be all-inclusive or reflect all the information about that article, provision, or description. Thus, it behooves the Principal, Agent, and all Third Parties to read the article, provision, or description carefully and with due diligence.

T: Governing Law: This CLPOA shall take effect immediately as a sealed instrument and shall receive interpretation, enforcement, and governance under the State's laws where the Principal has established physical residency at the time of enforcement. The Principal requests for the honoring of this CLPOA in any State, County, or Location in which the Principal's body or property may be, with the intention that it be valid in all jurisdictions/territories of the United States and all Foreign Nations. This CLPOA is to receive the most liberal interpretation available to grant the appointed Fiduciary the greatest amount of decision-making discretion.

1ˢᵗ **Witness:** _____   2ⁿᵈ **Witness:** _____   **Notary Public:** _____   **Principal:** _____

U: Severability / Saving Clause: An invalid or unenforceable provision within this CLPOA might exist. If that occurs, the remaining provisions of this CLPOA shall continue and be active as if said invalid or unenforceable provision did not exist. All remaining provisions shall be undisturbed to maintain their original legal meaning, force, and effect. If a court finds or deems that an invalidated or unenforceable provision will become valid if limitations exist, then such written provision shall receive a written modification by court order to limit the provision's power while maximizing the economic value and liberties granted.

V: Lapse of Time: A lapse of time shall not affect the validity or effectiveness of this CLPOA.

W: Legal Document Priority: If a court of competent jurisdiction appoints a Guardian or Conservator to oversee and manage the Principal's property, the Principal intended that this CLPOA take precedence over all other means of ascertaining the Principal's intentions. The Principal intends that this CLPOA shall not endure subjugation or subterfuge by any acting Guardian or Conservator unless the area in question is ambiguous. The Guardian or Conservator shall have wide latitude and discretion in their duties in ambiguous cases.

X: Court Appointed Guardian or Conservator: the Principal intends by this CLPOA to avoid a court-supervised guardianship or conservatorship. If the Principal attempts or fails to avoid a court-supervised guardianship or conservatorship. Then, the Principal requests that the Agent designated in this CLPOA serve as Guardian or Conservator of the Principal's property and affairs. The court-appointed Guardian or Conservator shall not have the power to revoke, suspend, or terminate this CLPOA or the Agent's powers except as specifically authorized by law. The Principal may execute the following: **"Declaration of Guardianship & Conservatorship,"** if execution occurs, the Principal prefers that those individuals act in such a fiduciary capacity.

Y: Specific Forms or In-House POA: If a Third Party refuses to recognize this CLPOA and requires a specific form or in-house Power of Attorney. The Agent can execute said legal document immediately subject to the limitations and rights established in this CLPOA with a permanent attachment of this CLPOA to said document.

Article XV: Acknowledgment by the Agent

A: The Agent shall exercise due care and act in the Principal's best interest with the powers granted while adhering to any limitations, impositions, or specifications within this CLPOA.

B: The Agent's foremost duty is loyalty and protection of the Principal and the Principal's interests. The Agent shall direct any benefits derived from this CLPOA to the Principal. The Agent must avoid conflicts of interest and use ordinary skill and prudence to exercise these powers. If there is anything about this CLPOA or the Agent's duties that the Agent does not understand, the Agent shall seek professional advice.

C: A court of competent jurisdiction has the discretion to revoke the Agent's power, especially if acting inappropriately. Thus, it behooves the Agent to exercise the bestowed powers in a fiduciary manner. The burden will be upon the Agent to prove that such acts were prudent and within a Fiduciary standard for any questionable acts. The Agent may be liable for damages and subject to criminal and civil prosecution if a court of competent jurisdiction finds that the Agent has violated their fiduciary duty.

D: The Agent has the power to abstain from using their granted powers under this CLPOA; however, the Agent does not have the luxury of being negligent when the **Life, Safety**, and **Welfare** of the Principal are at stake. The Agent may be liable for damages, be subject to prosecution (criminal or civil), and suffer termination of powers if a court rules that the Agent has been negligent regarding their fiduciary duty under this CLPOA to the Principal,

E: The Agent agrees to keep all monetary funds or financial assets that belong to the Principal in separate accounts from the Agent's monetary funds or financial assets. There shall be no commingling of monetary funds or financial assets to ensure simple accounting and safeguard the Principal's financial security. Furthermore, the Agent agrees to protect, conserve, and exercise prudence and caution in dealings with the Principal's monetary funds, financial assets, and all other assets of value and worth.

F: The Agent agrees to keep a complete/accurate record of all acts, disbursements, and receipts for review/inspection. The Agent agrees to provide an accounting/report to the Principal or Protector at the following time intervals (as stated below). If the Principal dies, the Executor/Administrator of the Principal's estate shall receive the accounting/report within a quarter. **Directions: Place a "✓" in the Accounting / Report Period box.**

Report Period: [ ] None   [ ] Monthly   [ ] Quarterly   [ ] Annually

1st **Witness:** _____   2nd **Witness:** _____   **Notary Public:** _____   **Principal:** _____

G: By default, the Agent shall not receive compensation for their authority, rights, and responsibilities; however, the Agent may receive reimbursement for reasonable and necessary expenses incurred in performing their authority, rights, and responsibilities. The Principal may compensate the Agent if the Principal desires.

H: The Agent shall disclose all actions that require written authorization by using their identity as the Agent in the following manner: (Agent's Signature) as Agent for (Principal's Name).

I: For Simple and Special POA, the Agent may resign by notifying the Principal or the Principal's Guardian or Conservator (provided a Judge appoints one). For Complex and Durable POA, the Agent may resign by notifying the Principal, Protector, Co-Agent, Successor Agent, or the Principal's Guardian or Conservator (provided a Judge appoints one). The resignation must be in writing and sent by certified mail, statutory overnight delivery (return receipt requested), or email.

J: If the Agent becomes aware of the death of the Principal who executed the CLPOA, the Agent must notify all Third Parties as soon as practicable that the Principal has died and that this CLPOA is no longer legitimate and effective. If Durability Provision(s) are not active or applicable, the Agent must notify all Third Parties as soon as practicable that the Principal is functioning non-socially, incapacitated, or incompetent; thus, the CLPOA is no longer valid.

K: If the Agent resigns or ceases to represent the Principal regarding this CLPOA, the former Agent agrees to return all property and documents to the Principal or the Protector (if **Article XII** is active).

L: The Agent agrees to keep all information (financial, relationship, or other personal matters) confidential and shall not disclose it to any outsiders unless those individuals are relevant Third Parties that require such information.

M: The Agent is responsible for informing the Principal of changes in their physical address or contact information.

N: If the Durable Provision(s) is active, the Agent may need to sign an Affidavit that the CLPOA is in Full Force and Effect to induce any Third Party to act.

O: The Agent understands that their power and rights are limited and shall be subservient to the Protector if **Article XII** is active. Upon request, the Principal or Protector shall provide the Agent with a copy of the Durable Protecting Power of Attorney, preferably by email as a PDF attachment.

P: If **Article XVI** is active, all Agents agree to implement the **Acknowledgment of Appointment by Agent** and proactively mail a copy to the Principal or Protector (if applicable).

Q: If **Article XVI** is active, all Agents wishing to resign shall fill out and sign the **Acknowledgment of Resignation by Agent** and proactively mail the original notarized Acknowledgment of Resignation by Agent to the Principal or Protector (if applicable).

O: The Agent understands that their power and rights are limited and shall be subservient to the Protector if **Article XII** is active. Upon request, the Principal or Protector shall provide the Agent with a copy of the Durable Protecting Power of Attorney, preferably by email as a PDF attachment.

Article XVI: Acknowledgment of Appointment by the Agent

SAFETY FEATURE: Implementing this option creates an administrative burden, but it also creates checks and balances. This option is a personal decision that the Principal must make for their future benefit.

Place "Y" for Yes or "N" for No in the box and initial "✐" the line if the Principal desires the following:

Requires Utilization of Acknowledgment of Appointment by Agent Form

"Y" or "N" Here ↑   Initial Here ↑

For brevity and consistency, the abbreviation of "Acknowledgment of Appointment by Agent" shall be "Appointment." By designating "Y" for Yes, the Principal requires the Agent to fill out, sign, and notarize the Appointment as a condition of becoming the acting Agent. The Agent shall forfeit their right to serve as an Agent by default if the Agent fails to implement the Appointment. The successor Agent shall become the current acting Agent, provided the successor Agent executes the Appointment. The appointment shall become a prerequisite for the Agent to implement in all succession matters. If the Principal selects a Co-Power Sharing for Agents, implementing this Appointment shall still be a requirement for each Agent. When utilizing the CLPOA with any Third Party, the Agent shall provide a copy of the Appointment to the Third Party. Failure to provide a copy of the Appointment to the Third Party shall result in the Third Party refusing and declining the CLPOA.

1st Witness: _____ 2nd Witness: _____ Notary Public: _____ Principal: _____

© 2018 by Paul M. Paquette; Form v3.00
All Rights Reserved; Paquette Publications

Complex Limited
Power of Attorney

You must verify the Agent's identity
with a government-issued picture I.D.

Page 13 of 16

Article XVII: Authorization of Delegation of Agent's Power to another Agent

SAFETY FEATURE: Implementing this option creates an administrative burden, but it also creates checks and balances. This option is a personal decision that the Principal must make for their future benefit.

Place "Y" for Yes or "N" for No in the box and initial "✐" the line if the Principal desires the following:

Delegation of Agent's Powers to another Agent

"Y" or "N" Here ↑   Initial Here ↑

By designating "Y" for Yes, the Principal allows delegating an Agent's powers to another Agent in **Article VII**. This discretionary power is useful when the acting Agent suffers inconveniences due to a lack of knowledge, logistics issues, or time constraints. The Agent who receives power from another Agent is the "Delegate." For transparency and record-keeping purposes, the utilization of the following forms shall occur: **"Delegation of Agent's Powers"** and **"Revocation of Delegate by (Agent, Principal, or Protector)"** with a copy mailed by the Agent to the Principal. If the Principal revokes an Agent, and the Agent has a Delegate, then the Delegate's powers are no longer active. If the Principal or Protector revokes an Agent due to a violation of Fiduciary duties, then that Agent shall not serve in the future as a Delegate. If the Principal or Protector revokes a Delegate for violating Fiduciary duties, then that Delegate shall not serve as an Agent forever.

Article XVIII: Security Footer Setting

SAFETY FEATURE: To prevent fraud and ensure legitimacy, the Principal may desire to enact a security feature known as the **"Security Footer."** Security Footer is burdensome; however, if the Principal believes that a party will contest or illegitimately alter this CLPOA, selecting the "High" setting may be desirable. The following pages will not usually have a security feature: (**01**) Cover Page, (**02**) Table of Contents, (**03**) Warning Page, (**04**) Informational Page, and (**05**) Intentionally blank separate page. The Principal requires the CLPOA to have the following security setting: **Directions: Place a "✓" in the Security Level box.**

Security Level: None   Low   Moderate   High

If the security selection is "**None**," no initial on the Security Footer is required. If the security selection is "**Low**," then the Principal's initial is required in the Security Footer. If the security selection is "**Moderate**," then the Principal's and Notary's initials are required in the Security Footer. If the security selection is "**High**," then the Principal's, Notary's, and Witness's initial is required in the Security Footer. The default option is "None" if the security selection is left blank (not "✓").

A: It might be suspicious if a page within this CLPOA lacks the necessary initials, as stated in the Security Footer setting indicated above. In this event, the whole page shall be invalid and deemed unenforceable.

B: If a Witness but not the other Witness (when (**02**) two Witnesses are required) forgot to initial the Security Footer, but the Notary and Principal initial that page, then that page shall survive **Article XVIII, Subsection A**. However, if no Notary's initial is present in the Security Footer and the Witness's initial is missing, then that page shall be subject to **Article XVIII, Subsection A**.

C: Under State Law, if this CLPOA is valid and enforceable with a Security Footer level of "Moderate," even though it is supposed to have a "High" Security Footer level." Then the following shall apply: If one or both Witnesses do not initial the Security Footer even though the Security Footer level is "High," then that page shall survive **Article XVIII, Subsection A**, providing that the Principal and Notary have initialed the page.

D: If the Security Footer requires a Notary's Initial and the Notary's Initial is not present, the page shall be subject to **Article XVIII, Subsection A**.

E: If the Security Footer requires a Principal's Initial and the Principal's Initial is not present, the page shall be subject to **Article XVIII, Subsection A**.

F: If a Witness is also a potential Health Care Surrogate, Mental Health Care Surrogate, Agent, Guardian, or Conservator, then due to conflict of interest, the Witness shall not serve in such a fiduciary capacity unless the Witness gets approval through a court of competent jurisdiction to act in a fiduciary role.

G: To prevent fraud, every revocation requires a Notary Initial, Signature, and Seal; one or more Witnesses are not required.

1st Witness: _____   2nd Witness: _____   Notary Public: _____   Principal: _____

Complex Limited
Power of Attorney

You must verify the Agent's identity
with a government-issued picture I.D.

Page 14 of 16

Article XIX: Ambiguities Interpretation Instructions

A: If a provision requires that a specific section be "Type" to be valid, failure to **"Type"** the section shall make that part invalid, null, and void.

B: If a provision requires that a specific section have the **Principal's Initial** for it to be valid, failure to initial the section shall make that part invalid, null, and void.

C: If a fillable section is **blank**, thus not typed or filled in, the legal interpretation shall be that the Principal did not intend for that section to be effective, and when it comes to interpreting that section, it shall be invalid, null, and void.

D: If a fillable section requires a **Yes "Y"** or **No "N"** and the section is blank (thus not typed or filled in), the legal interpretation shall be that the Principal did not intend for that section to be effective; therefore, it shall be **No "N."**

E: If a fillable section requires a **Yes "Y"** or No **"N;"** however, **"Yes"** or **"No"** exists instead, the legal interpretation shall be that the Principal did intend for that section to keep its legal effect and meaning.

F: If a fillable section requires a **Check "✓"** and it is blank, thus not typed or filled in, the legal interpretation shall be that the Principal did not intend for that section to be effective; therefore, not wanted.

G: If a fillable section gives multiple options that are mutually exclusive to each other in which a **Check "✓"** is required if more than one option is checked **"✓"** then the legal interpretation shall be that the Principal did this in error; thus when it comes to interpreting that section, the implementation shall be of the more conservative option.

H: If a fillable section requires a **Check "✓"** or "X," however a dash "—" exists instead, the legal interpretation shall be that the Principal did not intend for that section to be effective; thus, it is not wanted.

I: If a section or provision is typed with added handwritten instructions, only the "typed" section will receive consideration concerning the Principal's intentions. The rationale is simple: any person, not necessarily the Principal, can handwrite (ink in) after the fact. Due to a lack of verification, the additional handwritten instruction shall be invalid, null, and void.

J: Most state laws will void a legal document if someone writes on the surface, especially after notarization or execution. The Principal waives this right since the formalization of the CLPOA requires it to be typed and printed; thus, any handwritten alteration concerning the altered section shall be unsubstantial and nonbearing unless an unaltered original duplicate or legitimate copy is available; only the unreadable section shall be invalid, null, and void.

K: If this CLPOA allows handwritten statements by the Principal and there seem to be any suspicious alterations or additions (changes in handwriting style, changes in ink), such handwritten alterations or additions shall have no weight or bearing. Unless an unaltered original duplicate or legitimate copy is available, the altered section shall only be invalid, null, and void if it (the altered section) is unreadable as to its original intentions.

L: The Descriptions that follow a **Yes "Y"** or a **No "N"** Box are for clarification and informational purposes to outline the performance of duties and rights.

M: If a Third Party receives more than one active Power of Attorney regarding the Principal: **(01)** The Power of Attorney that has the most recent date shall take more precedence unless otherwise stated in **Article IX Subsection F**. **(02)** If the Principal function non-socially, incapacitated, or incompetent, then the Power of Attorney that has an active Durability Provision(s), in effect, shall take precedence. **(03)** If the Power of Attorney has the same date, then a General Power takes precedence over a Financial Power of Attorney. A Financial Power of Attorney takes precedence over a Banking Power of Attorney. A Limited Power of Attorney shall be subservient to a General, Financial, and Banking Power of Attorney if any conflicts arise. **(04)** A Protecting Power of Attorney shall stand alone and only be binding upon Complex and Durable Power of Attorney with active Protector provisions. **(05)** A Complex Power of Attorney takes precedence over a Simple Power of Attorney if any conflicts arise. **(06)** Unless otherwise specified within a Special Power of Attorney, a Special Power of Attorney shall take precedence over a Complex and Simple Power of Attorney if there are any conflicts.

Article XX: Signature and Execution

In the presence of (02) two Witnesses and a Notary, the Principal has executed this CLPOA. The Principal understands the full import and meaning of this CLPOA and is aware that this CLPOA gives the Agent **limited powers (written by the Principal) and ability regarding the Principal's property and affairs**. The Principal reaffirms the following in the Witnesses and Notary presence: (01) The Principal is at least eighteen (18) years or older. (02) The Principal is of sound and disposing mind (emotionally and mentally competent) to make or request this CLPOA. (03) The Principal has the capacity with full memory or necessary mental faculties to understand and comprehend these actions. (04) The Principal willfully and voluntarily executes this CLPOA. (05) The Principal declares under the Penalty of Perjury that this paragraph is true and correct.

| Principal → | Full Legal Name: | | Signature: | Thumb/Finger Print: |
| | Today's Date: | | | Real Estate Transaction |

Have (02) two Adult Witness* the Principal's signature in addition to having their signature notarized*

In the joint presence of each other, the Witnesses State that the Principal is the following: (01) The Principal is at least eighteen (18) years or older. (02) The Principal is of sound and disposing mind (emotionally and mentally competent). (03) The Principal is not suffering from constraint, duress, fraud, or undue influence. (04) The Principal acknowledges having willfully and voluntarily dated and signed this CLPOA (or asked/directed for such actions to occur). (05) The Witnesses affirm that they have no direct biological or marital relationship with the Principal and are not a Beneficiary of the Principal's estate. (06) The Witnesses affirm their impartiality and confirm that the criterion stated in the box at the bottom of the last page does not apply. (07) The Witnesses declare this paragraph true and correct under the Penalty of Perjury.

If the Witness is uncomfortable giving out personal contact information, current employment information and occupation will suffice.

1st Witness →	Name:		Signature:
	Address:		
	Phone #: Occupation:		Date:

2nd Witness Or Special Witness ** →	Name:		Signature:
	Address:		
	Phone #: Occupation:		Date:

1st Witness: _____ 2nd Witness: _____ Notary Public: _____ Principal: _____

Complex Limited
Power of Attorney

You must verify the Agent's identity
with a government-issued picture I.D.

Page 16 of 16

UNDER THE LAWS OF →

COUNTY: _____

STATE: _____

Before the Notary Public (the undersigned authority) comes forth, the Principal, with a sound/disposed mind, is eighteen (**18**) years or older. The Principal acknowledges having willfully and voluntarily dated and signed this CLPOA (or asked/directed for such actions to occur) stated above in the Notary Public presence. If Witnesses sign and attest that the Principal has signed this CLPOA, the Notary Public shall attest that the Witnesses have signed this CLPOA in the Notary Public's presence. Furthermore, the Notary Public states that the Principal has provided a Government Issue identification card with a facial picture to prove identity. The Notary Public declares under the Penalty of Perjury that this paragraph is true and correct.

If the Principal or Witnesses sign this CLPOA but not in the presence of the Notary Public, then the Notary Public will not notarize or sign this CLPOA.

* Notary Public →

Full Name:		Signature & Seal:
Location:		
Address:		
Phone #:		I.D. Number:
Date:		Commission Expires:

* None shall serve as a Witness, Notary Public, or other qualified individual with the authority to administer oaths regarding this CLPOA made under this section.

(**01**) Any individual related to the Principal by blood, marriage, or adoption. (**02**) Any individual currently a Beneficiary of the Principal's estate (laws of intestate succession or any existing will/codicil). (**03**) Any individual who benefits from a financial policy (insurance or annuity) in which the Principal's life is insured. (**04**) Any individual claiming (present/inchoate) any part of the Principal's estate. (**05**) Any individual who serves as an Owner, Operator, or employee of a Health Care Facility (Medical, Mental, or Assisted Living) in which the Principal is currently a Patient / Client unless the employee serves solely as a Notary Public. (**06**) Any Doctor, Physician, Psychologist, Psychiatrist, Social Worker, Financial Advisor, or Financial Manager in which the Principal is currently a Patient / Client. (**07**) Any individual who serves as an Owner, Operator, or employee of a Final Dispositional Facility (Funerary Home, Crematory Authority, and Cemetery Authority) unless the employee serves solely as a Notary Public. (**08**) Any individual who is an Agent (active/inactive) serving in a fiduciary capacity under this CLPOA. (**09**) Upon the Principal's death, any individual or entity with a claim (the creditor) against the Principal's estate. (**10**) Any individual under eighteen (**18**) years or is incapacitated or incompetent. The Witnesses should be twenty-one (**21**) years of age or older.

Special Witness** If the Principal is a resident of a sanitarium, rest home, nursing home, boarding home, et cetera, it is highly beneficial that a patient advocate or ombudsman be one of the Witnesses while executing this CLPOA.
Legal Questions: Consult the State laws or contact a licensed Attorney.

This page is intentionally left blank

This page is intentionally left blank

This page is intentionally left blank

This page is intentionally left blank

This page is intentionally left blank

This page is intentionally left blank

PUBLICATIONS

PAQUETTE

"The true man is revealed in difficult times." ~ Epictetus

Image Source

Broom Peddler – 1737 [1, 2 & 3]

Well Cleaner – 1746 [1 & 2]

Lettuce Seller – 1742 [1 & 2]

Hurdy-Gurdy Player – 1737 [1 & 2]

Fish Vendor – 1738 [1, 2 & 3]

Young Milkmaid – 1737 [1, 2 & 3]

Edmé Bouchardon [1]
Anne Claude Philippe [2]
Francois Joullain [3]

Black & White
Wood Engraving

Wikimedia
Commons

Image Source

Photo

"Love Family
Heart Parent"

Marcela

June 26, 2015

Photo ID: 826936

**CC License
from Pixabay**

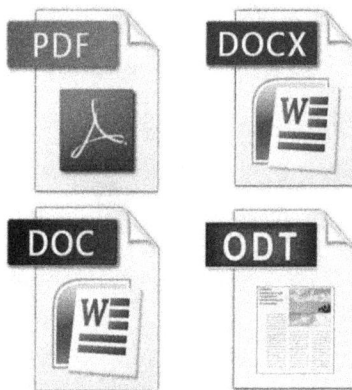

Graphic Art

(DOC, PDF, DOCX)

Jordan M. Groll

2008

(ODT)

Paul M. Paquette

2018

**Use with
Permission
Jgroll.com**

Graphic Art

**Star of Life
Blue Version**

**Rod of Asclepius,
with Snake around it**

Philippe Verdy

2006

**Wikimedia
Commons**

Graphic Art

**Paquette
Publications**

Logo by

Paul M. Paquette

2018

Image Source

Photo

Corey Seeman

Aug 01, 2010

St. Clair Flats South
Channel Range Lights
(Lake St. Clair,
Michigan)

CC License
through Flickr

- **Simple POA** is for short-term (less than five years) use with an Agent whose honor is beyond reproach and doubt. The Simple POA has only one additional (**01**) option/safety feature: **Durability Provision**, hence the name "**Simple**." If Durability Provisions are active, this POA will also qualify as a "**Durable POA**."

  - **Key Details:** Names only one Agent, Effective Immediately, Define Expiration Date, and Built-In Safety Features
  - **Option:** Durability Provisions

- **Complex POA** is for long-term (greater than five years) use, preferably with multiple Agents to reflect the changing realities of life. These multiple options/safety features, if implemented, will create an administrative burden by establishing checks and balances on the Agent's power, hence the name "**Complex**." If Durability Provisions are active, this POA will also qualify as a "**Durable POA**." If Springing Power(s) are active, this POA will also qualify as a "**Springing POA**."

  - **Key Details:** Names Multiple Agent with successor's Agent, Variable Effective Date, Variable Expiration Date, Built-In Safety Features, and Sprinkling Powers
  - **Options:** Durability Provisions, Springing Powers, Agent Co-Power Sharing, Protector Provision, Delegate Provision, and Security Footer Settings.

- **Durable POA** is, in essence, a Complex POA, but with one key difference: the Durability Provisions are already active; thus, the durability provision is a "Key Detail" instead of an "Option." By default, the Durable POA will never have a simpler version due to the nature of the subject matter. This POA qualifies as a "**Durable POA**." If Springing Power(s) are active, this POA will also qualify as a "**Springing POA**."

- **Special POA** is, in essence, a Simple POA, best used sparsely with a limited scope and purpose. By default, the Special POA will never have a more complex version due to the nature of the subject matter. If Durability Provisions are active, this POA will also qualify as a "**Durable POA**." This POA is also referenced as a "**Limited POA**."

Power of Attorney

Simple Banking Power of Attorney

Power of Attorney (POA only)
for Your Estate Planning Needs

(Requires Internet)
Downloadable Files

Paul M. Paquette

Preview the entire book in advance
at www.Legal-POA.com

Complex Banking Power of Attorney

Power of Attorney (POA only)
for Your Estate Planning Needs

(Requires Internet)
Downloadable Files

Paul M. Paquette

Preview the entire book in advance
at www.Legal-POA.com

Simple Financial Power of Attorney

Power of Attorney (POA only)
for Your Estate Planning Needs

(Requires Internet)
Downloadable Files

Paul M. Paquette

Preview the entire book in advance
at www.Legal-POA.com

Complex Financial Power of Attorney

Power of Attorney (POA only)
for Your Estate Planning Needs

(Requires Internet)
Downloadable Files

Paul M. Paquette

Preview the entire book in advance
at www.Legal-POA.com

Power of Attorney

1st Edition
Abridged Version

Visual Forms within are intended for Illustration Purposes

PP ™

Simple General Power of Attorney

Power of Attorney (POA only)
for Your Estate Planning Needs

(Requires Internet)
Downloadable Files

Paul M. Paquette

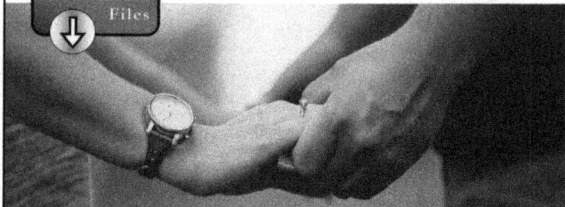

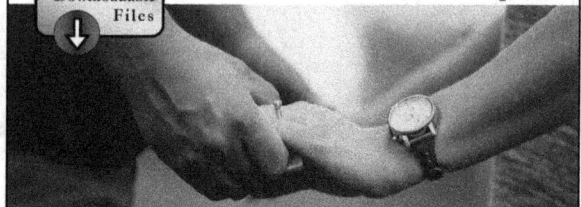

Preview the entire book in advance
at www.Legal-POA.com

1st Edition
Abridged Version

Visual Forms within are intended for Illustration Purposes

PP ™

Complex General Power of Attorney

Power of Attorney (POA only)
for Your Estate Planning Needs

(Requires Internet)
Downloadable Files

Paul M. Paquette

Preview the entire book in advance
at www.Legal-POA.com

1st Edition
Abridged Version

Visual Forms within are intended for Illustration Purposes

PP ™

Simple Limited Power of Attorney

Power of Attorney (POA only)
for Your Estate Planning Needs

(Requires Internet)
Downloadable Files

Paul M. Paquette

Preview the entire book in advance
at www.Legal-POA.com

1st Edition
Abridged Version

Visual Forms within are intended for Illustration Purposes

PP ™

Complex Limited Power of Attorney

Power of Attorney (POA only)
for Your Estate Planning Needs

(Requires Internet)
Downloadable Files

Paul M. Paquette

Preview the entire book in advance
at www.Legal-POA.com

Power of Attorney

Simple Real Estate Power of Attorney

Power of Attorney (POA only)
for Your Estate Planning Needs

(Requires Internet)
Downloadable Files

Paul M. Paquette

Preview the entire book in advance
at www.Legal-POA.com

Complex Real Estate Power of Attorney

Power of Attorney (POA only)
for Your Estate Planning Needs

(Requires Internet)
Downloadable Files

Paul M. Paquette

Preview the entire book in advance
at www.Legal-POA.com

Simple Power of Attorney for Minor Child

Power of Attorney (POA only)
for Your Estate Planning Needs

(Requires Internet)
Downloadable Files

Paul M. Paquette

Preview the entire book in advance
at www.Legal-POA.com

Complex Power of Attorney for Minor Child

Power of Attorney (POA only)
for Your Estate Planning Needs

(Requires Internet)
Downloadable Files

Paul M. Paquette

Preview the entire book in advance
at www.Legal-POA.com

Power of Attorney

Durable Protecting Power of Attorney

Power of Attorney (POA only)
for Your Estate Planning Needs

(Requires Internet)
Downloadable Files

Paul M. Paquette

Preview the entire book in advance
at www.Legal-POA.com

Durable Power of Attorney for Final Disposition (Funeral & Burial)

Power of Attorney (POA only)
for Your Estate Planning Needs

(Requires Internet)
Downloadable Files

Paul M. Paquette

Preview the entire book in advance
at www.Legal-POA.com

Durable Power of Attorney for Health Care

Power of Attorney (POA only)
for Your Estate Planning Needs

(Requires Internet)
Downloadable Files

Paul M. Paquette

Preview the entire book in advance
at www.Legal-POA.com

Durable Power of Attorney for Health Care of Minor Child

Power of Attorney (POA only)
for Your Estate Planning Needs

(Requires Internet)
Downloadable Files

Paul M. Paquette

Preview the entire book in advance
at www.Legal-POA.com

Power of Attorney

Declarations

Declaration of Guardianship & Conservatorship

Legal Forms for your Estate Planning Needs
with Supporting Documents

(Requires Internet) Downloadable Files

Paul M. Paquette

Preview the entire book in advance
at PaquettePublications.com

Declaration of Guardianship & Conservatorship for Minor Child

Legal Forms for your Estate Planning Needs
with Supporting Documents

(Requires Internet) Downloadable Files

Paul M. Paquette

Preview the entire book in advance
at PaquettePublications.com

Declaration of Guardianship & Conservatorship for the Disabled

Legal Forms for your Estate Planning Needs
with Supporting Documents

(Requires Internet) Downloadable Files

Paul M. Paquette

Preview the entire book in advance
at PaquettePublications.com

Declaration of Final Disposition (Funeral & Burial)

Legal Forms for your Estate Planning Needs
with Supporting Documents

(Requires Internet) Downloadable Files

Paul M. Paquette

Preview the entire book in advance
at PaquettePublications.com

Declarations

Declaration of Health Care (Living Will)

Legal Forms for your Estate Planning Needs with Supporting Documents

(Requires Internet)
Downloadable Files

Paul M. Paquette

Preview the entire book in advance at PaquettePublications.com

Declaration of Organs & Tissues Donation (Anatomical Gifts)

Legal Forms for your Estate Planning Needs with Supporting Documents

(Requires Internet)
Downloadable Files

Paul M. Paquette

Preview the entire book in advance at PaquettePublications.com

Advance Directives

Advance Medical Health Directive

Legal Forms for your Estate Planning Needs
with Supporting Documents

(Requires Internet)
Downloadable Files

Paul M. Paquette

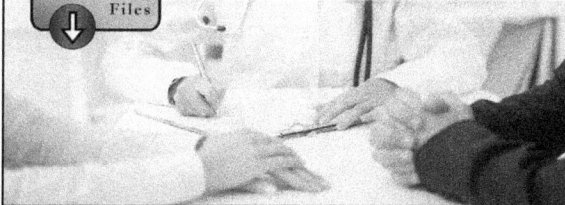

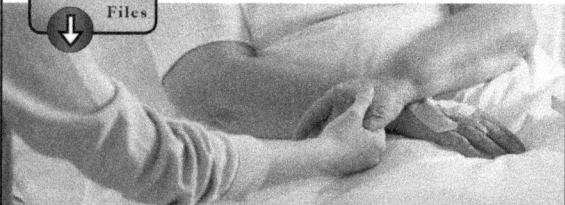

Preview the entire book in advance
at PaquettePublications.com

Advance Mental Health Directive

Legal Forms for your Estate Planning Needs
with Supporting Documents

(Requires Internet)
Downloadable Files

Paul M. Paquette

Preview the entire book in advance
at PaquettePublications.com

Do Not Resuscitate Advance Directive (DNR)

Legal Forms for your Estate Planning Needs
with Supporting Documents

(Requires Internet)
Downloadable Files

Paul M. Paquette

Preview the entire book in advance
at PaquettePublications.com

Relationship Agreements

Prenuptial Agreement

Legal Forms for your Estate Planning Needs
with Supporting Documents

(Requires Internet)
Downloadable Files

Paul M. Paquette

Preview the entire book in advance
at PaquettePublications.com

Postnuptial Agreement

Legal Forms for your Estate Planning Needs
with Supporting Documents

(Requires Internet)
Downloadable Files

Paul M. Paquette

Preview the entire book in advance
at PaquettePublications.com

Prenuptial Agreement
For Same-Sex Marriage

Legal Forms for your Estate Planning Needs
with Supporting Documents

(Requires Internet)
Downloadable Files

Paul M. Paquette

Preview the entire book in advance
at PaquettePublications.com

Postnuptial Agreement
For Same-Sex Marriage

Legal Forms for your Estate Planning Needs
with Supporting Documents

(Requires Internet)
Downloadable Files

Paul M. Paquette

Preview the entire book in advance
at PaquettePublications.com

Relationship Agreements

1st Edition
Visual Forms within are intended for Illustration Purposes

Prenuptial Agreement
for Civil Union / Partnership

Legal Forms for your Estate Planning Needs
with Supporting Documents

(Requires Internet)
Downloadable Files

Paul M. Paquette

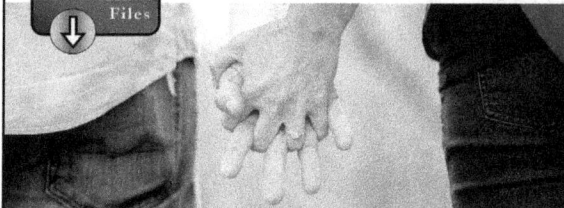

**Preview the entire book in advance
at PaquettePublications.com**

1st Edition
Visual Forms within are intended for Illustration Purposes

Postnuptial Agreement
for Civil Union / Partnership

Legal Forms for your Estate Planning Needs
with Supporting Documents

(Requires Internet)
Downloadable Files

Paul M. Paquette

**Preview the entire book in advance
at PaquettePublications.com**

1st Edition
Visual Forms within are intended for Illustration Purposes

Custodial Agreement
for Minor Child

Legal Forms for your Estate Planning Needs
with Supporting Documents

(Requires Internet)
Downloadable Files

Paul M. Paquette

**Preview the entire book in advance
at PaquettePublications.com**

1st Edition
Visual Forms within are intended for Illustration Purposes

Visitation Agreement
for Minor Child

Legal Forms for your Estate Planning Needs
with Supporting Documents

(Requires Internet)
Downloadable Files

Paul M. Paquette

**Preview the entire book in advance
at PaquettePublications.com**

Relationship Agreements

Guardianship Agreement for Minor Child

Legal Forms for your Estate Planning Needs with Supporting Documents

(Requires Internet) Downloadable Files

Paul M. Paquette

Preview the entire book in advance at PaquettePublications.com

Guardianship Agreement for Disabled Adult

Legal Forms for your Estate Planning Needs with Supporting Documents

(Requires Internet) Downloadable Files

Paul M. Paquette

Preview the entire book in advance at PaquettePublications.com

Cohabitation Agreement

Legal Forms for your Estate Planning Needs with Supporting Documents

(Requires Internet) Downloadable Files

Paul M. Paquette

Preview the entire book in advance at PaquettePublications.com

Domestic Partnership Agreement

Legal Forms for your Estate Planning Needs with Supporting Documents

(Requires Internet) Downloadable Files

Paul M. Paquette

Preview the entire book in advance at PaquettePublications.com

Relationship Agreements

Separation Agreement

1st Edition — Visual Forms within are intended for Illustration Purposes

Legal Forms for your Estate Planning Needs with Supporting Documents

(Requires Internet) Downloadable Files

Paul M. Paquette

Preview the entire book in advance at PaquettePublications.com

Reconciliation Agreement

1st Edition — Visual Forms within are intended for Illustration Purposes

Legal Forms for your Estate Planning Needs with Supporting Documents

(Requires Internet) Downloadable Files

Paul M. Paquette

Preview the entire book in advance at PaquettePublications.com

Word Processor Program

The Purchaser or User can open, edit, print, and save the Digital Files using a word processing program. Popular Word Processing Programs include Microsoft Word, WordPerfect, Open Office, and Libre Office. All word processing forms come in the following (**DOC, DOCX, ODT**). Paquette Publications does not offer the Word Processing Program or Technical Support for the Word Processor Program.

Portable Document Format (PDF) Editor

The Purchaser or User can open, edit, print, and save the Digital Files using a PDF Editor program. Popular PDF Editor include Adobe Acrobat Pro, Nitro Pro 11, PDF-Xchange Editor, Master PDF Editor, and CutePDF Writer. Paquette Publications does not offer the PDF Editor or Technical Support for the PDF Editor. Adobe Acrobat Reader is free to download at www.adobe.com. **Please Note:** due to encryption standards of **256-bit AES**, this PDF is only backward compatible (read/write) with **Adobe Acrobat X or later**.

Printer Setting

Depending on the printer's capabilities and settings, the Digital File (**DOC, DOCX, ODT**) may need editing to prevent cut-off text from occurring near the margins. The easiest way to solve this problem is to verify that the printer and margin settings are correct. If you still have issues, edit/fill out the Digital File, convert it, and save it as a **PDF** file. PDF files are easier, more versatile, and present fewer errors when printing. Paquette Publications does not offer Printing capabilities or Technical Support for Printers.

Modification Recommendation

If the Purchaser or User plans to make changes to the Digital File in question, it is highly advantageous that the Purchaser or User utilize the (**DOC, DOCX, or ODT**) file format. If the Purchaser or User is content with the choice selection, provisions, and options currently available with minor changes (if applicable), then it is highly recommended that the Purchaser or User utilize the **PDF** file format.

Downloadable Digital Files

Legal Disclaimer:

The Forms presented in this Book are available as a direct download from **www.paquettepublications.com**. In adherence with **Copyright Laws**, **Licensing Agreements**, and **Legal Disclaimers & Waivers**, these forms and their files are for personal and immediate family use only.

Legal Disclaimer required by the Distributor:

This Book does not have digital files (**PDF**, **DOCX**, **DOC**, and **ODT**) attached and does not contain fillable files or forms. As a courtesy, the Author has provided an Active URL Link to download the digital file (**PDF**, **DOCX**, **DOC**, **ODT**); however, the Purchaser or User will need to have an internet service connection, computer access, appropriate software, printing capabilities, and the ability and willingness to access the Author's website.

File Format Options:

The Digital Files are in the following formats: Microsoft Office Word (**DOC**, **DOCX**), Adobe Acrobat (**PDF**), and Open Office (**ODT**). The **PDF**, **DOCX**, **DOC**, and **ODT** are fillable and editable with the appropriate computer software.

Consent Checkbox:

To download these Digital Files (**PDF**, **DOCX**, **DOC**, and **ODT**), the Purchaser or User must first consent to the following Terms and Conditions (**Legal Disclaimer & Waivers**, **Licenses & Trademark**, and **All Rights Reserved**) which are present on the website.

Terms & Conditions

> ☐ **By checking this box, the Purchaser or User has read and agree to the following:** Legal Disclaimers & Waivers, License & Trademark, **and** All Rights Reserved **before downloading these file(s) (PDF, DOCX, DOC, ODT).**
>
> submit

Download Links:

Using an internet browser (**Chrome**, **Edge**, **Explorer**, **Firefox**, and **Safari**), the Purchaser or User can download the Forms (**PDF**, **DOCX**, **DOC**, and **ODT**) presented within this Book from the following active URL Links:

Power of Attorney:
- https://paquettepublications.weebly.com/tc---cpoa28---poa33.html

Supporting Documents:
- https://paquettepublications.weebly.com/agrave-la-carte.html

Worksheets:
- https://paquettepublications.weebly.com/agrave-la-carte.html

Forms (Miscellaneous):
- https://paquettepublications.weebly.com/agrave-la-carte.html

Forms (Recommended):
- https://paquettepublications.weebly.com/agrave-la-carte.html

Appendices & Glossary:
- https://paquettepublications.weebly.com/free---appendix.html

Extras:
- https://paquettepublications.weebly.com/free---extra.html

CD / DVD

This CD / DVD is designed (built and formatted) to work with Microsoft's Windows Operating System but should also work on Apple's Macintosh Operating System. **Please Note:** Paquette Publications does not provide technical support for computers or operating systems.

Print on Demand (POD) book
will have no CD / DVD available.

Please refer to the **"Downloadable
Digital Files"** page to access the file(s)
(PDF, DOCX, DOC, and ODT).

Please Return Disc with Book

www.ingramcontent.com/pod-product-compliance
Lightning Source LLC
Chambersburg PA
CBHW051228200326
41519CB00025B/7288